Anonymous

**List of Selected Ancient Monuments in the Madras
Presidency**

Anonymous

**List of Selected Ancient Monuments in the Madras Presidency**

ISBN/EAN: 9783337384845

Printed in Europe, USA, Canada, Australia, Japan

Cover: Foto ©ninafisch / pixelio.de

More available books at **www.hansebooks.com**

# LIST

OF

# ANCIENT MONUMENTS

### SELECTED FOR CONSERVATION

IN THE

## MADRAS PRESIDENCY.

Revised up to 12th December 1910.

MADRAS:

PRINTED BY THE SUPERINTENDENT, GOVERNMENT PRESS.

1911.

# INTRODUCTION.

---

THE present edition of the list of Ancient Monuments selected for conservation in the Madras Presidency is the third of the kind, the first one having been issued by Dr. Burgess in 1886–87 and the second by myself in 1891. It is issued under the authority of Government conveyed in G.O., No. 513, Public, dated 13th June 1910. The number of monuments in the present list has increased enormously and it must be admitted that with further investigation some more additions will have to be made.

A map showing the localities where the monuments are situated has been put in with a view that visitors may have facilities for recognising the sites, and ascertain whether they are on the Railway line or out of it, and in the latter case to know the probable distance therefrom. In some places, the numbers of monuments are too numerous for all their names to be inserted in the map—Vijiyanagar and the Seven Pagodas are examples of such sites—and these can only be ascertained by referring to the body of the list.

The appendices have been purposely inserted with a view to their being of service to the officials of the Public Works and Revenue Departments in dealing with archæological works. They contain most of the information that may have to be consulted in the discharge of the duties connected with all Ancient Monuments.

Lastly it must be admitted that owing to numerous difficulties, it is not always possible to overlook the possibility of error in the preparation of such a list. So I shall feel much obliged if any inaccuracies noticed by others are kindly communicated to me in order that they may be duly corrected, and that when necessary, a revised edition, free from such errors, may be issued.

ALEXANDER REA.

BANGALORE, }
13th July 1910. }

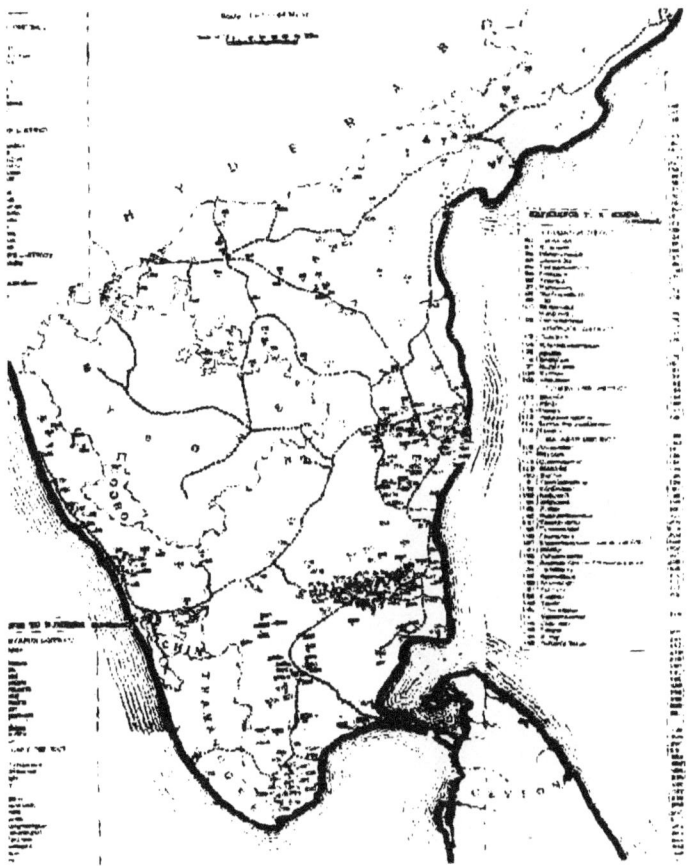

# LIST OF SELECTED ANCIENT MONUMENTS IN THE MADRAS PRESIDENCY.

## REVISED UP TO 12TH DECEMBER 1910.

[N.B.—Those printed in italics are only included provisionally, and their permanent retention will be subject to further consideration.]

| Serial number. | Taluk. | Village. | Name of monument. | Reason for conservation. | Government or private; and, if latter, whether funds are available or not. | Remarks showing 'protected,' etc. |
|---|---|---|---|---|---|---|
| | | | **FIRST CIRCLE (P.W.D.).** | | | |
| | | | GANJÁM DISTRICT. | | | |
| 1 | Berhampur. | Jogada | Asoka rock inscription | Historical | Government. | |
| 2 | Chicacole | Chicacole | Jumma Musjid | Architectural | Private (no funds). | |
| 3 | Goomsur | Kottakolla | Gangadarasvami and Jagadesvarasvami temples on Bagada hill. | Archæological. | Do. | Protected. |
| 4 | *Sompeta Agency.* | *Mahendragiri.* | *Four temples and cross* | *Do.* | *Private.* | |
| | | | VIZAGAPATAM DISTRICT. | | | |
| 5 | Anakápalle. | Sankaram | Buddhist monolithic and structural remains of a monastery on the Bojannakonda hills. | Archæological. | Zamindari | Protected. |
| 6 | Vizianagram | Hamatirtham. | Buddhist structural remains of a monastery on the Bodikonda, Gurubaktbakonda and Durgakonda hills. | Do. | Do. | Do. |
| 7 | Do. | Kannimitta-agraharam. | Somakondan with an inscription | Historical | | |
| 8 | Do. | Saripalli | Deserted temple | Archæological. | Zamindari | Protected. |
| 9 | *Vizagapatam.* | *Simhachellem* | *Vishnu temple* | *Do.* | *Private (has funds).* | |
| 10 | *Do.* | *Darlakonda* | *Buddhist remains on hill* | *Do.* | *Zamindari.* | |
| | | | GÓDÁVARI DISTRICT. | | | |
| 11 | *Amalápuram.* | *Polavaram* | *Two ancient temples* | *Archæological* | *Zamindari.* | |
| 12 | *Pithápuram.* | *Chendurti* | *Buddhist remains on hill near Chandavolu.* | *Do.* | *Do.* | |
| 13 | Rajahmundry. | Rajahmundry. | Mosque | Do. | Private | Protected. |
| 14 | Ramachandrapuram. | Draksharamam. | Bhimesvara temple and inscription | Archæological and Historical. | Do. | |
| 15 | *Yellavaram* | *Jaddangi* | *Cave temple* | *Archæological.* | *Do.* | |
| | | | **SECOND CIRCLE (P.W.D.).** | | | |
| | | | KISTNA DISTRICT. | | | |
| 16 | *Bezwada* | *Bezwada* | *Malesvara temple with inscriptions.* | *Archæological and Historical.* | *Private.* | |
| 17 | Do. | Do. | Ali Hussain Durga | Archæological. | Private (no funds). | |
| 18 | Do. | Do. | Cave, west of Bezwada | Do. | Government. | |
| 19 | Do. | Do | Mallikarjuna temple | Do. | Private (has funds). | |
| 20 | Do. | Do. | Nagaresvara temple on the hill side. | Do. | Government. | |
| 21 | Do. | Do. | Rock cuttings on the hill, including five caves. | Do. | Do. | |
| 22 | Do. | Kondura | Narasimhasvami temple | Do. | Private. | |
| 23 | Do. | Kondapalli. | Hill fort and palace on the hill | Historical | Government. | |
| 24 | Do. | Mogalrajapuram. | Caves on the hill | Archæological. | Do. | |
| 25 | Bunder | Ghuntasala. | Jalalesvarasvami and Visvesvarasvami temple. | Do. | Private (no funds). | |
| 26 | Do. | Do. | Ruined Buddhist stupa in mound. | Do. | Private. | |
| 27 | Do. | Bunder | Dutch cemetery | Historical | Government. | |
| 28 | Ellore | Adamalle | Stone images | Archæological. | Do. | |
| 29 | Do. | Guntapalle. | Buddhist chaityas and stupas and all the rock cut caves. | Do. | Zamindari (no funds). | |
| 30 | Do. | Pedavegi | Mounds covering the ancient site of the Telugu Kings of Kengi. | Do. | Government. | |
| 31 | Gudiváda | Gudiváda | Langa dibba with remains of Buddhist stupa and the ancient village-site. | Do. | Do. | |

| Serial number. | Taluk. | Village. | Name of monument. | Reason for conservation. | Government or private; and, if latter, whether funds are available or not. | Remarks showing 'protected,' etc. |
|---|---|---|---|---|---|---|

## SECOND CIRCLE (P.W.D.)—cont.

### KISTNA DISTRICT—cont.

| | | | | | | |
|---|---|---|---|---|---|---|
| 32 | Gudivâda .. | Gudivâda .. | Siva temple with Jaina image and inscription. | Archæological and Historical. | Private (no funds). | |
| 33 | Nandigama. | Jaggayya-petta. | Buddhist remains of a stupa on the hill. | Archæological. | Government. | |
| 34 | Narasapur .. | Palakollu .. | Dutch cemetery and inscriptions .. | Archæological and Historical. | Do. | |
| 35 | Yernagudem | Arulla .. | Remains of viharas and stupas in mounds. | Archæological. | Do. | |

### GUNTÚR DISTRICT.

| | | | | | | |
|---|---|---|---|---|---|---|
| 36 | Bâpatla . | Bâpatla .. | All the inscriptions in the temple of Bhava Narainasvami. | Historical .. | Private (no funds). | Protected. |
| 37 | Do. .. | Chinna Ganjám. | Chidambarasvami temple .. | Archæological. | Do. | |
| 38 | Do. .. | Do. | Ruins of Buddhist stupa in a mound. | Do. | .... | |
| 39 | Do. .. | Motupalli .. | Buddhist remains at Sakaladanidibba. | Do. | Government. | |
| 40 | Do. .. | Do. .. | Chola temple with inscriptions .. | Archæological and Historical. | Private (no funds). | Protected. |
| 41 | Do. .. | Pedda Ganjám. | Bogandani dibba with remains of a stupa. | Archæological. | Private. | |
| 42 | Do. .. | Do. | Bhava Narainasvami temple .. | Do. | Private (no funds). | |
| 43 | Do. .. | Santaravora. | Chinuakesvaperumal temple .. | Do. | Do. | |
| 44 | Do. .. | Do. | Ramalingasvami and Nagesvara temple. | Do. | Do. | |
| 45 | Guntúr .. | Sitanagaram. | Rock-out caves on the hill .. | Do. | Government. | |
| 46 | Do. .. | Vundavalli. | Four-storeyed rock-cut cave .. | Do. | Do. | |
| 47 | Do. .. | Do. | Isvara temples . .. .. | Do. | Do. | |
| 48 | Narasaraopet | Chejorla .. | Kopatesvara temple with a Chaitya used as shrine and some marble sculptures. | Do. | Private. | |
| 49 | Ongole .. | Kannaparti.. | Buddhist white marble sculptures lying in the village. | Do. | Do. | |
| 50 | Do. .. | Do. .. | Isvara temple .. .. .. | Do. | Private (no funds). | |
| 51 | Do. .. | Do. .. | Mounds .. .. .. .. | Do. | Government. | |
| 52 | Sattenapalle. | Amaravati.. | Amaresvara temple .. .. | Do. | Private (has funds). | |
| 53 | Do. | Do. .. | Mound containing a Buddhist stupa and other remains. | Do. | Government. | |
| 54 | Do. | Do. .. | Fort of Daranikota .. | Do | Do. | |
| 55 | Do. | Do. .. | Inscriptions on rock, west of Daranikota. | Historical .. | Do. | |
| 56 | Do. | Bellamkonda. | Hill fort with its buildings .. | Do. .. | Do. | |
| 57 | Do. | Daranikota. | Buddhist and other remains in Kuchi dibba and Nakka dibba. | Archæological. | Do. | |
| 58 | Do. | Garikapadu. | Buddhist stupa with sculptures in a mound. | Do. | Private (has funds). | |
| 59 | Do. | Panidem .. | Mounds .. .. .. .. | Do. | Do. | |
| 60 | Tanali .. | Bhattiprolu. | Lanpa dibba with remains of a stupa. | Do. | Government. | |
| 61 | Vinukonda .. | Vinukonda .. | Three hill forts with their buildings and inscriptions. | Historical .. | Do. | |

### NELLORE DISTRICT.

| | | | | | | |
|---|---|---|---|---|---|---|
| 62 | Atmakur .. | Anomasamudram. | Fakir's tomb .. .. | Archæological .. | Government. | |
| 63 | Darsi .. | Kochavlakota. | Old fort .. .. .. | Historical .. | Do. | |
| 64 | Kanigiri .. | Kanigiri .. | Hill fort .. .. .. | Do. .. | Do. | |
| 65 | Nellore .. | Nellore .. | Irckulamma and Darmaraja temples. | Archæological. | Private (has funds). | |
| 66 | Do. .. | Do. .. | Renganayakula temple .. | Do. | Do. | |

## 3

| Serial number | Taluk. | Village. | Name of monument. | Reason for conservation. | Government or private; and, if latter, whether funds are available or not. | Remarks showing 'protected,' etc. |
|---|---|---|---|---|---|---|
| | | | **SECOND CIRCLE (P.W.D.)—cont.** | | | |
| | | | **NELLORE DISTRICT—cont.** | | | |
| 67 | Nellore .. | Nellore .. | Mulasthaneswara temple .. .. | Historical .. | Private (has funds). | |
| 68 | Do. .. | Do. .. | Fort.. .. .. .. | Do. .. | Government. | |
| 69 | Polar .. | Kondaveda. | Hill fort with lines of fortifications and other buildings. | Do. .. | Do. | |
| 70 | Do. .. | Do. | Vishnu temple .. .. .. | Archaeological .. | Private. | |
| 71 | Rapur .. | Rapur .. | Old fort with remains of palace, etc. | Historical .. | Government. | |
| 72 | Udayagiri .. | Udayagiri .. | Hill fort with all ancient enclosed buildings. | Do. .. | Do. | |
| 73 | Do. .. | Do. .. | Bompanayakulu temple .. .. | Archaeological .. | .... | |
| 73A | Do. .. | Daseripalli. | Cave .. .. .. .. | Do. .. | .... | |
| | | | **THIRD CIRCLE (P.W.D.).** | | | |
| | | | **ANANTAPUR DISTRICT.** | | | |
| 74 | Anantapur. | Anantapur. | Sir Thomas Munroe's house and the two wells dug by him. | Historical .. | Government. | |
| 75 | Gooty .. | Gooty .. | Fort and its buildings including also the fortification at the foot of the hills. | Do. | Do. | |
| 76 | Do. .. | Uravakonda. | Mallikarjunaswami temple .. | Archaeological. | Private (no funds). | |
| 77 | Hindupur .. | Gorantla .. | Madhavaragani temple .. | Do. | Private. | |
| 78 | Do. .. | Lepakshi .. | Virabhadraswami temple .. | Do. | Private (no funds). | |
| 79 | Do. .. | Do. .. | Basavannah (Bull) .. | Architectural. | Government. | |
| 80 | Kalyandrug. | Kambaduru. | Sira temple .. .. | Archaeological. | Private (has funds). | |
| 81 | Do. | Pobbarlapalli. | Ruined mandapam and well .. | Do. | Do. | |
| 82 | Madakasira. | Hemavati .. | Sculptures on and near the ancient site. | Do. | .... | |
| 83 | Do. | Madakasira. | Hill fort .. .. .. | Historical .. | Government. | |
| 84 | Do. | Do. | Two large bastions and gateway (remains of the fortified wall which enclosed the old town). | Do. .. | Do. | |
| 85 | Do. | Retnagiri .. | Fort enclosing granary, well, etc. | Do. .. | Private (no funds). | |
| 86 | Pennkonda. | Bukkapatnam. | Palace .. .. .. | Architectural. | Government. | |
| 87 | Do. | Kalipi .. | Ramaswami temple .. | Archaeological. | Private (no funds). | |
| 88 | Do. | Penukonda. | Five ancient wells .. | Do. | Government. | |
| 89 | Do. | Do. | Pasurakeri well .. | Do. .. | Private. | |
| 90 | Do. | Do. | Abdul Hussain Mosque .. | Architectural. | Private (has funds). | |
| 91 | Do. | Do. | Fort .. .. | Historical .. | Government. | |
| 92 | Do. | Do. | Gabana mahal .. | Architectural and Archaeological. | Do. | |
| 93 | Do. | Do. | Iswara temple .. | Architectural. | Private (no funds). | |
| 94 | Do. | Do. | Two detached pavillions in the field. | Architectural and Archaeological. | Government. | |
| 95 | Do. | Do. | Ancient gopuram .. | Architectural. | Do. | |
| 96 | Do. | Do. | Rama's bastion .. | Historical .. | Do. | |
| 97 | Do. | Do. | Kalchatti Gutta .. | Do. .. | Do. | |
| 98 | Do. | Do. | Tombs near the palace .. | .... | .... | |
| 99 | Do. | Do. | Ramaswami temple .. | Architectural | Private (no funds). | |
| 100 | Do. | Do. | Sher Ali's mosque.. .. | Do. | Private (has funds). | |
| 101 | Tadpatri .. | Chukkaluru. | Obinnakeswara temple .. | Do. | Private (no funds). | |
| 102 | Do. .. | Tadpatri .. | Chintalarayaswami temple .. | Do. | Private .. | Protected. |
| 103 | Do. .. | Do. .. | Ramaswami temple .. | Archaeological. | Do. .. | Do |

1-A

4

| Serial number | Taluk. | Village. | Name of monument. | Reason for conservation. | Government or private; and, if latter, whether funds are available or not. | Remarks showing 'protected,' etc. |
|---|---|---|---|---|---|---|

### THIRD CIRCLE (P.W.D.)—*cont.*

#### BELLARY DISTRICT.

| | | | | | | |
|---|---|---|---|---|---|---|
| 104 | Adóni | Adóni | Jamma Masjid | Architectural. | Private. | |
| 105 | Do. | Do. | Fort and the buildings contained therein. | Historical | Government. | |
| 106 | Do. | Peddathumbalam. | Ramasvami temple | Archæological. | Private. | |
| 107 | Do. | Do. | Ruins of Kalkautharayan temple. | Do. | .... | |
| 108 | Alur | Venkatapuram. | Raganathasvami temple on Malayavandan hill. | Do. | Private. | |
| 109 | Do. | Chippagiri | Bhojesvara temple | Do. | Do. | |
| 110 | Do. | Do. | Chinnakesavasvami temple | Do. | Do. | |
| 111 | Do. | Do. | Jain temple on the hill | Du. | Do. | |
| 112 | Bellary | Bellary | Hill fort | Historical | Government. | |
| 113 | Harpanahalli. | Bagali | Kallesvara temple | Architectural. | Private (no funds). | |
| 114 | Do. | Halvagalu | Kallesvara temple | Archæological. | Private. | |
| 115 | Do. | Do. | Mallikarjuna temple | Architectural. | Do. | |
| 116 | *Do.* | *Harpanahalli.* | *Poligar hill fort* | *Historical* | *Do.* | |
| 117 | Do. | Kuruvatti | Mallikarjunasvami temple | Architectural. | Do. | |
| 118 | Do. | Nilagunda | Bhimesvara temple | Do. | Private (no funds). | |
| 119 | *Do.* | *Uchchangidurgam.* | *Hill fort and palace* | *Historical* | *Do.* | |
| 120 | Hadagalli | Huvinahadagalli. | Fort | Do. | Government. | |
| 121 | Do. | Do. | Kallesvara temple | Architectural. | Private (no funds). | |
| 122 | *Do.* | *Rangapuram.* | *Narasimmasvami temple* | *Archæological* | *Do.* | *Protected.* |
| 123 | Do. | Hirehadagalli. | Kallesvara temple | Do. | Private. | |
| 124 | Do. | Magalam | Suryanarayanasvami temple | Do. | Government. | |
| 125 | Do. | Mailara | Kattesvara temple | Do. | Private. | |
| 126 | Hospet | Anantasayanagudi. | Large ruined temple | Architectural. | Government. | |
| 127 | Do. | Melapanagudi. | Well (Snlaibhavi) | Archæological. | .... | |
| 128 | Do. | Hospet | Jambunada temple | Do. | Private (no funds). | |
| 129 | Do. | Do. | Muhammadan tombs outside the town. | Do. | Government. | |
| 130 | Do. | Timmalapuram. | Siva temple | Do. | Do. | Protected. |
| 131 | Do. | Do. | Gopalakrishnasvami temple | Do. | Do. | Do. |
| 132 | Do. | Hampi | All the ancient deserted remains. | Archæological and Architectural. | Do. | |
| 133 | Do. | Do. | Achutanarayanasvami temple | Architectural. | Do. | |
| 134 | Do. | Do. | Ganigatta temple near Kamalapuram. | Do. | Do. | |
| 135 | Do. | Do. | Hazari Ramasvami temple with sculptures and fort walls. | Do. | Do. | |
| 136 | Do. | Do. | Jain temple, south of Pampapathi temple. | Do. | Do. | |
| 137 | Do. | Do. | Krishnasvami temple | Do. | Do. | |
| 138 | Do. | Do | Malayavanta Ragunatha temple | Do. | Do. | Protected. |
| 139 | Do. | Do. | Monolithic statue of Narasimha | Do. | Do. | |
| 140 | Do. | Do. | Pampapathi temple | Do. | Private. | |
| 141 | Do. | Do. | Pattabiramasvami temple | Do. | Government. | |
| 142 | Do. | Do. | Ramasvami temple | Archæological. | Private. | |
| 143 | Do. | Do. | Vittalasvami | Architectural. | Government. | |
| 144 | Kadligi | Ambali | Kallesvara temple | Archæological. | Private. | |
| 145 | *Rayadrug* | *Rayadrug* | *Extensive hill fortress with its outlying fortifications, palace and two temples of Rama and Krishna.* | *Archæological and Historical.* | *Government.* | |

| Serial number. | Taluk. | Village. | Name of monument. | Reason for conservation. | Government or private; and, if latter, whether funds are available or not. | Remarks showing 'protected.' etc. |
|---|---|---|---|---|---|---|
| | | | **THIRD CIRCLE (P.W.D.)**—cont. | | | |
| | | | **CUDDAPAH DISTRICT.** | | | |
| 146 | Cuddapah | Cuddapah | Nawab's towers at the Jail | Archaeological | Government. | |
| 147 | Do. | Do. | Old well near the tower | Do. | Do. | |
| 148 | Do. | Do. | Four ancient mosques in the town | Do. | Private. | |
| 149 | Do. | Do. | Temples on the Pushpagiri hill | Do. | Private (no funds). | Protected. |
| 150 | Do. | Sivalpalli | Visvanathasvami temple | Do. | Private | Do |
| 151 | Jammalamadugu | Danavulapadu | Remains of buried Jain temple | Do. | Government. | |
| 152 | Do. | Gandikotta | Fort with the enclosed ancient buildings | Historical | Do. | |
| 153 | Do. | Do. | Tower known as "Madorasala". | Do. | Do. | |
| 154 | Do. | Do. | Madhavaperumal temple | Archæological. | Private. | |
| 155 | Do. | Peddamudiyam. | Ranganadhasvami temple | Do. | Do. | |
| 156 | Do. | Do. | Mukantesvara temple | Do. | Do. | |
| 157 | Do. | Do. | Narasimhasvami temple | Do. | Do. | |
| 158 | Do. | Do. | Old Vishnu temple with inscriptions. | Archæological and Historical. | Do. | |
| 159 | Do. | Do. | Ancient village-site | Archæological. | Government. | |
| 160 | Madanapalle. | Sompalle | Vishnu temple and dvajasthambam. | Archæological and Architectural. | Private. | |
| 161 | Pullampet | Attorala | Deserted temple of Parasurama | Architectural. | Government. | |
| 162 | Do. | Nandaluru | Saumyanadasvami temple | Archæological. | Private (has funds). | |
| 163 | Siddhavattam. | Siddhavattam. | Ancient galleried well by roadside | Do. | Government. | |
| 164 | Do. | Joti | Ruined Vishnu temple | Do. | Do. | |
| 165 | Do. | Do. | Old Sidesvarasvami temple | Do. | Private. | |
| 166 | Do. | Near Joti | Ancient remains | Do. | Do. | |
| 167 | Do. | Siddhavattam | Fort with the ancient buildings enclosed therein. | Historical | Government. | |
| 168 | Do. | Rajampet | Ancient well ' Bogandanibavi' | Archæological. | Do. | Protected. |
| 169 | Do. | Vontimitta. | Kothandaramasvami temple | Archæological and Architectural. | Private. | |
| 170 | Vayalpad | Gurramkonda | Fort | Historical | Government. | |
| 171 | Do. | Do. | Mahal | Architectural. | Do. | |
| 172 | Do. | Do. | Narasimmasvami temple | Archæological. | Private. | |
| | | | **KURNOOL DISTRICT.** | | | |
| 173 | Cumbum | Cumbum | Old Muhammadan tomb | Architectural | Private. | |
| 174 | Do. | Krishnamsettipalle. | Bimesvara temple | Archæological | Do. | |
| 175 | Nandikothur. | Allotta | Fort and ruins of a town | Historical | Do. | |
| 176 | Do. | Srisailam | Temple with inscriptions | Archæological and Historical. | Private (has funds). | |
| 177 | Nandyal | Mahanandi | Mahanandesvara temple | Archæological. | Private. | |
| 178 | Ramallakot | Kurnool | Mussalman fort | Historical | Do. | |
| 179 | Do. | Do. | Tombs of Abdulla Wahab Khan. | Architectural | Do. | |
| 180 | Sirvel | Ahobilam | Group of temples known as the Nava Narasimha with inscriptions. | Archæological and Historical. | Do. | |
| 181 | Do. | Digwa Ahobilam. | Large mandapam | Architectural. | Do. | |

| Serial number. | Taluk. | Village. | Name of monument. | Reason for conservation. | Government or private ; and, if latter, whether funds are available or not. | Remarks showing 'protected,' etc. |
|---|---|---|---|---|---|---|

## FOURTH CIRCLE (P.W.D.).

### COIMBATORE DISTRICT.

| | | | | | | |
|---|---|---|---|---|---|---|
| 182 | Bhavani .. | Bhavani .. | Sangameswarmswami temple .. | Archæological. | Private (has funds). | |
| 183 | Coimbatore. | Perur . | Temple .. .. .. .. | Do. | Do. | |
| 184 | Dhárápuram. | Padiyar .. | Badrakali Amman temple .. | Do. | Private (no funds). | |
| 185 | Erode .. | Vijayamangalam. | Jain temple .. .. | Do. | Do. | Protected. |
| 186 | Do. .. | Sarkar Periyapalaiyam. | Temple on the tank .. .. | Historical .. | Do. | |
| 187 | Karúr .. | Tandoni .. | Rock-cut carvings representing Renganadhaswami and Narayanaswami with inscriptions. | Archæological and Historical. | Government .. | Protected. |

### MALABAR DISTRICT.

| | | | | | | |
|---|---|---|---|---|---|---|
| 188 | Calicut .. | Annasheri | Narayanaperumal temple .. | Archæological. | Private. | |
| 189 | Do. .. | Beypore .. | Siva temple .. .. | Do. | Do. (has funds). | |
| 190 | Do. .. | Do. .. | Old fort .. .. .. | Historical .. | Do. | |
| 191 | Do. .. | Choruvannur | Narayanamurti temple .. | Archæological. | Do. | |
| 192 | Do. .. | Elakkad .. | Ganapathi temple .. | Do. | Do. | |
| 193 | Do. . | Elattur .. | Bhagavati temple .. | Do. | Do. | |
| 194 | Do. .. | Kaniparamba | Temple .. .. .. | Do | Do. | |
| 195 | Do. .. | Karamballi. | Subramaniaswami temple .. | Do. | Do. | |
| 196 | Do. .. | Koduvalli .. | Sankaramurti temple .. | Do | Do. | |
| 197 | Do. .. | Do. .. | Santhanagopalaswami temple | Do. | Do. | |
| 198 | Do. .. | Do. .. | Narasimhamurti temple . | Do. | Do. | |
| 199 | Do. .. | Do. .. | Narasimhaswami temple .. | Do. | Do. | |
| 200 | Do. .. | Mayanad .. | Siva temple .. .. | Do | Do | |
| 201 | Do. .. | Do. .. | Vishnu temple .. .. | Do | Do. | |
| 202 | Do. .. | Pottur .. | Narasimhamurti temple .. | Do. | Do. | |
| 203 | Do. .. | Padinattumori. | Siva temple .. | Do. | Do. | |
| 204 | Do .. | Talakolattur. | Narasimhaswami temple .. | Do. | Do. | |
| 205 | Do. .. | Tiruvambadi. | Subramaniaswami temple .. | Architectural. | Do. | |
| 206 | Chirakkal .. | Cannanore .. | Dutch fort .. .. .. | Historical .. | Government. | |
| 207 | Do. .. | Kunjomangalam. | Mosque .. .. .. | Archæological .. | Private. | |
| 208 | Do. .. | Madayi .. | Mosque founded in 1124 A.D. | Do. .. | Do. | |
| 209 | Do. .. | Do. .. | Old Eli palace .. .. | Do. .. | Do. | |
| 210 | Do. .. | Mount D'Eli. | Remains of the fort .. | Historical .. | Do. | |
| 211 | Do. .. | Takparamba. | Siva temple .. .. | Archæological .. | Do. | |
| 212 | Kottayam .. | Tellicherry.. | Fort .. .. .. | Do. .. | Government. | |
| 213 | Palghat .. | Agathaithara. | Ancient temple .. .. | Do. .. | Private (has funds). | |
| 214 | Do. .. | Kavacheri .. | Temple .. .. .. | Architectural. | Do. | |
| 215 | Do. .. | Pallavur .. | Siva temple .. .. | Archæological and Architectural. | Private. | |
| 216 | Do. .. | Palghat .. | Ancient Jain temple .. | Archæological. | Do. | |
| 217 | Do. .. | Do. .. | Fort .. .. .. | Historical .. | Government. | |
| 218 | Do. .. | Thinarai .. | Isvara temple .. .. | Do. .. | Do. | |
| 219 | Do. . | Tiruvalathur. | Bhagavathi temple .. | Architectural. | Do. | |
| 220 | Do. .. | Vadakkamseri. | Siva temple .. .. | Architectural and Archæological. | Do. | |
| 221 | Poonáni .. | Chalisseri .. | Two Ancient Syrian Churches | Architectural .. | Do. | |
| 222 | Do. .. | Toriyar .. | An Ancient Syrian Church .. | Do. .. | Do. | |
| 223 | Walavanad. | Kovur .. | Krishnamurti temple .. | Archæological. | Do. | |
| 224 | Do. .. | Do. .. | Kanneswaraswami temple .. | Do. .. | Do. | |
| 225 | Wynad .. | Sultan's Battery. | Jain temple .. .. .. | Do. .. | .. . | |

| Serial number | Taluk. | Village. | Name of monument. | Reason for conservation. | Government or private; and, if latter, whether funds are available or not. | Remarks showing protected, etc. |
|---|---|---|---|---|---|---|

**FOURTH CIRCLE (P.W.D.)—cont.**

**NILGIRI DISTRICT.**

| | | | | | | |
|---|---|---|---|---|---|---|
| 226 | Coonoor .. | Hallikaldrug | Fort .. .. .. .. | Historical .. | Government. | |
| 227 | Do. .. | R'Ladiuru. | Group of sculptured cromlechs .. | Do. | Do. | |
| 228 | Ootacamund. | Mekkundah .. | Sculptured cromlechs .. .. | Archæological .. | .... | |

**NORTH ARCOT DISTRICT.**

| | | | | | | |
|---|---|---|---|---|---|---|
| 229 | Arcot .. | Arcot .. | Delhi Gate .. .. .. | Historical .. | Government. | |
| 230 | Do. .. | Kulamandal. | Vishnu temple at Ukkal .. .. | Archæological. | Do. | |
| 231 | Do. .. | Mamandur. | Rock-cut caves, sculptures and inscriptions. | Do. | Do. | |
| 232 | Do. .. | Narasapala-yam. | Rock-cut caves .. .. .. | Do. | Do. | |
| 233 | Do. .. | Pudupadi .. | Baradwajesvara temple .. .. | Do. | Private (no funds). | |
| 234 | Do. .. | Do. .. | Vedanarayana Perumal temple .. | Do. | Do. | Protected. |
| 235 | Do. .. | Panchapan-davamalai. | Rock-cut sculptures and caves .. | Do. | Government. | |
| 236 | Do. .. | Ukkal .. | Vishnu temple .. .. | Do. | Private. | |
| 237 | Arni .. | Devika-puram. | Brihadambal temple .. .. | Do. | Private (has funds). | |
| 238 | Do | Do. | Kanakagoresvara temple .. .. | Do. | Do. | |
| 239 | Chendragiri. | Tirupati .. | Two gopurams on the Tirupati hills (large gopuram at the foot of the hills—Gali gopuram at the top). | Do. | Do. | |
| 240 | Do. | Do. .. | Srinivasaperumal temple .. | Do. | Do. | |
| 241 | Do. | Do. .. | Alamelumangal temple .. .. | Do. | Do. | Partly renewed. |
| 242 | Do. | Chendragiri. | Fort with its buildings on the hill and the lower one with the two palaces. | Archæological and Historical. | Government. | |
| 243 | Do. | Timmapuram. | Ruined temple, one mile east of Chendragiri. | Archæological. | .... | |
| 244 | Chittoor .. | Erukampet. | Perumal temple .. .. .. | Do. | Private. | |
| 245 | Do. .. | Melpadi .. | Somanada temple .. .. .. | Architectural. | Government. | |
| 246 | Do. .. | Do. | Cholesvara temple .. .. | Archæological. | Do. | |
| 247 | Do. .. | Vallimalai .. | Jain sculptures and inscriptions on the hill. | Archæological and Historical. | Do. | |
| 248 | Do. .. | Do. .. | Subramaniasvami temple .. | Historical .. | Private. | |
| 249 | Gudiyattam. | Tiruvellam. | Bilhanadesvara temple .. .. | Archæological. | Do. | |
| 250 | Do. | Satghar .. | Seven Hill Forts .. .. | Historical .. | | |
| 251 | Kalahasti Division. | Tirumala-puram. | Konar temple .. .. .. | Archæological. | Private (no funds). | |
| 252 | Polur .. | Gangasallur. | Gangesvara temple .. .. | Do. | Do. | |
| 253 | Do. .. | Tirumalai .. | Jaina rock-cut caves, sculptures and mandapams with paintings and inscriptions. | Archæological and Historical. | Do. | |
| 254 | Do. .. | Padaved .. | Hanumar temple .. .. | Do. | .... | |
| 255 | Punganur .. | Laddiyam .. | Temple .. .. .. | Archæological. | Private (has funds). | |
| 256 | Do. .. | Miniki .. | Minikibanda rock .. .. | Do. | Do. | |
| 257 | Tiruttani .. | Tiruttani .. | Temple of Subramanya .. | Do. | Private. | |
| 258 | Vellore .. | Abdullapu-ram. | Abdul Mahal .. .. . | Architectural. | Government. | |
| 259 | Do. .. | Nelvoy .. | Ramasvami temple .. .. | Archæological. | Private. | |
| 260 | Do. .. | Vellore .. | Fort .. .. .. | Archæological and Historical. | Government. | |
| 261 | Do. .. | Do. .. | Jalakantesvara temple .. .. | Architectural. | Do. | |

| Serial number | Taluk. | Village. | Name of monument. | Reason for conservation. | Government or private; and, if latter, whether funds are available or not. | Remarks showing 'protected,' etc. |
|---|---|---|---|---|---|---|

## FOURTH CIRCLE (P.W.D.)—cont.
### NORTH ARCOT DISTRICT—cont.

| | | | | | | |
|---|---|---|---|---|---|---|
| 262 | Vellore .. | Virinjipuram. | Margasakayesvara temple .. | Archæological. | Private. | |
| 263 | Do. .. | Veppampattu | Siva temple .. .. .. | Do. | Do. | |
| 263a | Do. .. | Sholapuram. | Do. .. .. .. | Historical .. | Do. | |
| 264 | Wallajapet. | Mahendravadi. | Monolithic rock-cut temple .. | Do. .. | Government. | |
| 265 | Do. | Sholingar .. | Narasimhasvami temple .. .. | Do. .. | Private. | |
| 266 | Do. | Do. .. | Nachiar temple .. .. .. | Do. .. | Do. | |
| 267 | Do. | Do. .. | Padmapuram temple .. .. | Do. .. | Do. | |
| 268 | Do. | Do. .. | Sanjivirayasvami temple .. ̈ .. | Do. .. | Do. | |
| 269 | Do. | Do. .. | Rock inscription in the right flank of Sholingar tank. | Do. .. | .... | |
| 270 | Wandiwash. | Siyamangalam. | Rock-cut temple and sculptures .. | Do. .. | Private (no funds). | |
| 271 | Do. | Tellar .. | Isvara temple .. .. .. | Do. .. | Do. | |
| 272 | Do. | Wandiwash. | Fort .. .. .. .. | Do. .. | Government. | |

### SALEM DISTRICT.

| | | | | | | |
|---|---|---|---|---|---|---|
| 273 | Krishnagiri. | Krishnagiri. | Hill fort .. .. .. | Archæological. | Government. | |
| 274 | Do. | Royakottai .. | Do. .. .. .. | Historical | .... | |
| 275 | Namakkal .. | Namakkal .. | Fort and buildings on the hill | Historical and Archæological. | Government. | |
| 276 | Salem .. | Taramangalam. | Siva temple .. .. .. | Archæological. | Do. | |
| 277 | Tiruchengode. | Sankaridrug. | Fort and temple on the hill .. | Historical and Archæological. | Do. | |

### SOUTH CANARA DISTRICT.

| | | | | | | |
|---|---|---|---|---|---|---|
| 278 | Kasaragod.. | Bekal .. | Fort .. .. .. .. | Historical .. | Government. | |
| 279 | Do. .. | Hossadrug. | Hill fort .. .. .. | Do. | .... | |
| 280 | Mangalore .. | Gurpur .. | Rajah's palace known as the 'Matham' with fine carvings. | Historical and Architectural. | .... | |
| 281 | Do. .. | Mangalore.. | Mangaladevi temple .. .. | Archæological. | Private (no funds). | |
| 282 | Do. .. | Do. .. | Sultan's battery, three miles north of Mangalore. | Historical .. | Private. | |
| 283 | Do. .. | Mudbidri .. | Old Jain Basti, pillars in the tombs of the Jain priest. | Archæological and Architectural. | Do. | |
| 284 | Do. ... | Venur .. | Jain statue, 35 feet high, and three Jain bastis. | Archæological. | Private (no funds). | |
| 285 | Udipi .. | Karkala .. | Jain statue "Gumtesvara Devi." | Do. | Do. | |
| 286 | Do. .. | Do. | Jain temple "Chadurmuka Basti." | Do. | Do. | |
| 287 | Do. .. | Halsaugudi. | Great sthamba .. .. .. | Do. | Do. | |
| 288 | Uppinangudi. | Guruvayankuri. | Jain temple mandapam and sthambs. | Do. | Do. | |
| 289 | Do. | Jammalabad. | Rock fort .. .. .. | Historical .. | Do. | |

## FIFTH CIRCLE (P.W.D.).
### CHINGLEPUT DISTRICT.

| | | | | | | |
|---|---|---|---|---|---|---|
| 290 | Chingleput. | Arapakam .. | Jain images .. .. .. | Archæological. | Private (no funds). | |
| 291 | Do. | Do. .. | Siva temple .. .. .. | Architectural. | Private. | |
| 292 | Do. | Chingleput | 'Ther Mahal' used as sub-jail within the Reformatory School. | Do. | Government. | |
| 293 | Do. | Mamallapuram. | All the rock-cut and ancient structural remains. | Archæological. | Do. | |
| 294 | Do. | Orakadam .. | Vadamalesvarar temple .. .. | Do. | Private. | |
| 295 | Do. | Sadras .. | Ruined fort and cemetery .. | Historical .. | Government. | |

# 9

| Serial number | Taluk. | Village. | Name of monument. | Reason for conservation. | Government or private; and, if latter, whether funds are available or not. | Remarks showing 'protected,' etc. |
|---|---|---|---|---|---|---|

## FIFTH CIRCLE (P.W.D.)—cont.

### CHINGLEPUT DISTRICT—cont.

| | | | | | | |
|---|---|---|---|---|---|---|
| 296 | Chingleput.. | Salavankuppam. | Caves and rock .. .. .. | Archæological. | Private. | |
| 297 | Do. .. | Tirukalikunram. | Orukal mantapam .. .. | Do. | Do | |
| 298 | Do. .. | Tiruvadanthai. | Nityakalyana Bavanaguswami temple. | Do | Private (no funds). | |
| 299 | Do. .. | Vayalur .. | Tirupuleswara temple and inscriptions. | Archæological and Historical | Private. | |
| 300 | Conjeeveram. | Tenneri .. | Large Siva temple .. | Archæological. | Do. .. | Protected. |
| 301 | Do. | Do. .. | Lesser Siva temple .. | Do. | Do. .. | Do. |
| 302 | Do. | Conjeeveram | Airavateevara temple .. , .. | Do. | Do. | |
| 303 | Do. | Do. | Jvarahareevara temple .. .. | Do. | Private (no funds). | Is being renewed. |
| 304 | Do. | Do. | Kailasanatha temple .. | Archæological dates about 500 A.D. | Private .. | Protected. |
| 305 | Do. | Do. | Tiruparanthakeevara temple .. | Archæological. | Do. | |
| 306 | Do. | Do. | Kamatchi Amman temple .. | Do. | Private (has funds). | |
| 307 | Do. | Do. | Kachapeevara temple .. .. | Do. | Private (no funds). | |
| 308 | Do. | Do. | Matangeevara .. .. | Do | Do. | |
| 309 | Do. | Do. | Vardaraja Perumal temple .. | Do. | Private. | |
| 310 | Do. | Do. | Muktesvara .. .. | Do. | Do. | |
| 311 | Do. | Do. | Vaikuntaperumal temple .. | Do. | Do. .. | Protected. |
| 312 | Do. | Sriperambudur. | Budaparceevarar temple .. .. | Do. | Private (no funds). | |
| 313 | Do. | Do. | Vishnu temple .. .. .. | Do. | Private (has funds). | |
| 314 | Do. | Kuram .. | Pandavaperumal temple .. | Do. | Private (no funds). | |
| 315 | Do. | Manimangalam. | Old temple with a apidal gopuram. | Do. | Private .. | Protected |
| 316 | Do. | Do. | Vaikuntavaraleeperuma- temple .. | Do. | Do. | |
| 317 | Do. | Somangalam. | Somanataswami temple .. .. | Do. | Do. | |
| 318 | Do. | Triuparatikunram. | Jain temple .. .. .. | Do. | Private (no funds). | Protected. |
| 319 | Madurantakam. | Kadamalaiputtur. | Cromlechs in and out of the forest reserve at the foot of Perumbair hills. | Do. | Government reserve. | |
| 320 | Do. | Perumbair.. | Tandaneevar temple .. .. | Do. | Government. | |
| 321 | Ponnéri .. | Pulicat .. | Dutch cemetery in the fort .. | Historical .. | .... | |
| 322 | Saidapet .. | Little Mount. | Rock-cut cave under the church.. | Traditionally the site of St. Thomas' Martyrdom. | Private (has funds). | |
| 323 | Do. .. | Pallávaram. | Mounds and prehistoric sites on the hills. | Archæological. | Government. | |
| 324 | Do. .. | Do. | Cave on the Panchapandava hill. | Do. | Private. | |
| 325 | Do. .. | Do | Siva temple at Tirusulam .. | Do. | Private (no funds). | |
| 326 | Do. .. | St. Toomas' Mount. | Cross in the church on the hill .. | Do | Do. | |
| 327 | Tiruvallur .. | Kumbakkam.. | Remains of hill fort with palaces and other buildings. | Historical .. | .... | |
| 328 | Do. .. | Tiruvallur .. | Vishnu Temple .. .. .. | Archæological. | Private. | |

### MADRAS DISTRICT.

| | | | | | | |
|---|---|---|---|---|---|---|
| 329 | Madras .. | Madras .. | Old Town well .. .. .. | Historical .. | Government. | |
| 330 | Do. .. | Do. .. | Cornwallis Memorial (near the Customs House, Madras). | Do. .. | Do. | |

2

FIFTH CIRCLE (P.W.D.)—cont.

SOUTH ARCOT DISTRICT.

| Serial number. | Taluk. | Village. | Name of monument. | Reason for conservation. | Government or private ; and, if latter, whether funds are available or not. | Remarks showing 'protected,' etc. |
|---|---|---|---|---|---|---|
| 331 | Chidambaram. | Chidambaram. | Siva temple.. .. .. .. | Archæological. | Private (has funds). | Partly renewed. |
| 332 | Do. | Sirimuahnam. | Buvaragaavami temple .. .. | Do. | Do. | |
| 333 | Do. | Do. | Nitisvaraswami temple .. | Do. | Do. | |
| 334 | Cuddalore .. | Cuddalore .. | Remains of Fort St. David with old tombs, etc. | Historical .. | Government. | |
| 335 | Kallakurichi. | Tiyagar .. | Rock fortress .. .. .. | Do. .. | .... | |
| 336 | Tindivanam. | Chittamur .. | Jain temple .. .. .. | Archæological. | Private (has funds.) | |
| 337 | Do. | Ginjee .. | Fortress comprising a hill-fort on the Rajagiri, an inner and a lower fort, and lines of fortifications connecting the Rajagiri, Krishnagiri and Chakkili Durgam (Orme's St. George's Mountain) hills. In and about the fortress are the following objects. | Archæological and Historical. | Government. | |
| 338 | Do. | Do. .. | On the Rajagiri—Two granaries, a magazine, flagstaff, Ranganatha's temple, Kamalakkanni Amman's temple and the sacrificial slab in front of it, a big cannon, a treasury and an audience hall. | Do. | Do. | |
| 339 | Do. | Do. .. | On the Krishnagiri—Two granaries, well for storing ghee, well for storing oil, two temples and an audience chamber. | Do. | Do. | |
| 340 | Do. | Do. .. | In the inner and lower forts—(a) Inner fort—A granary, a gymnasium, Kalyanamahal, stables and barracks, and Anaikkulam tank. (b) Lower fort—Chakkarnikulam and Chettikulam ponds, idol of Hanuman, Sadat Alla Khan's mosque with Persian inscriptions, inscription in Persian on Pondicherry gate (A.D. 1713), Venkatramanaswami temple, prisoners' well and old jail near the Arcot gate. | Do. | Do. | |
| 341 | Do. | Do. .. | Outside the fort—(1) Pattabhiramaswami temple in Narasingarayanpettai. (2) Twelve-pillared mantapam in Narasingarayanpettai. (3) Twenty-four Jain figures on Thiruvathavunu in Sirukadambur. | Do. | Do. | |
| 342 | Do. | Kunimedu .. | Remains of early English factory known as ' Conimere.' | Historical .. | Do. | |

■

| Serial number | Taluk. | Village. | Name of monument. | Reason for conservation. | Government or private; and, if latter, whether funds are available or not. | Remarks showing 'protected,' etc. |
|---|---|---|---|---|---|---|

## FIFTH CIRCLE (P.W.D.)—cont.

### SOUTH ARCOT DISTRICT—cont.

| | | | | | | |
|---|---|---|---|---|---|---|
| 343 | Tindivanam. | Melaicheri.. | Siva temple .. .. .. | Archæological. | Private (no funds). | |
| 344 | Do. | I.e. .. | Ruined fort and palace and rock-cut temple on hill south of the village. | Historical .. | .... | |
| 345 | Do. | Tondur .. | Rock-cut caves and couches on Panchapandavarmalai hill. | Archæological.. | .... | |
| 346 | Do. | Singavanam. | Renganadasvami temple .. | Do. .. | Private (no funds). | |
| 347 | Tirukovilur .. | Arukandanallur. | Siva temple with rock-out caves .. | Do .. | .... | |
| 348 | Tiruvannámalai. | Tiruvannamalai. | Siva temple on the hill .. .. | Do. .. | Private .. | Partly renewed. |
| 349 | Do. | Do. | Eight old Muhammadan tombs .. | Do. .. | .... | |
| 350 | Villupuram. | Mandagappattu. | Sculptured rock-cut mandapam on the hill. | Do. .. | .... | |

### TANJORE DISTRICT.

| | | | | | | |
|---|---|---|---|---|---|---|
| 351 | Kumbakónam. | Kumbakónam. | Kasivisvanadhasvami temple .. | Archæological. | Private (has funds). | |
| 352 | Do. | , Do. | Kumbesvarasvami temple .. | Do. | Do. | |
| 353 | Do. | Do. | Somesvarasvami temple .. .. | Do. | Do. | |
| 354 | Do. | Do. | Nagesvarasvami temple .. | Do. | Do. | |
| 355 | Do. | Do. | Ramasvami temple .. .. | Do. | Do. | |
| 356 | Do. | Do. | Sarangapanisvami temple .. | Do. | Do. | |
| 357 | Do. | Do. | Mahamaha tank .. .. | Do. | Do. | |
| 358 | Do. | Do. | Banapurisvara temple .. .. | Do. | Do. | |
| 359 | Do. | Do. | Chakrapaniswami temple .. | Do. | Do. | |
| 360 | Do. | Do. | Mallikarjunaswami temple .. | Do. | Do. | |
| 361 | Do. | Tiruvalanjali. | Svetavinayagasvami temple .. | Do. | Do. | |
| 362 | Do. | Tirukkalittattai. | Vedapurisvara temple .. .. | Do. | Do. | |
| 363 | Do. | Tiruppanandal. | Isvara temple .. .. .. | Do. | Private | |
| 364 | Do. | Tiruvisanallur. | Sivayoganathaswami temple .. | Do. | Do. | |
| 365 | Do. | Do. | Karkatesvarar temple ..: .. | Do. | Do. | |
| 366 | Do. | Svamimalai. | Svaminadasvami temple .. | Historical .. | Do. .. | Partly renewed. |
| 367 | Do. | Darasaram. | Airavatesvara temple .. | Archæological. | Private (no funds). | |
| 368 | Do. | Tiruvidamarudur. | Mahalingasvami temple .. | Do. | Do. | Is being renewed. |
| 369 | Máyavaram. | Tranquebar. | Dansborg Castle .. .. | Archæological and Historical. | Government .. | Protected. |
| 370 | Do. | Máyavaram. | Mayuranathasvami temple .. | Archæological .. | Private (has funds). | Is being renewed. |
| 371 | Do | Do. | Vellalarkoil temple .. | Do. .. | Do. | |
| 372 | Mannárgudi. | Nidámangalam. | Subterranean passage .. | Do. .. | Do. | |
| 373 | Negapatam. | Negapatam. | Dutch cemetery .. .. .. | Historical .. | Government. | |
| 374 | Do. | Do. | Nilakthakshiyamman temple .. | Archæological. | Private (has funds). | |
| 375 | Do. | Tiruvalúr .. | Large Siva temple .. .. | Archæological and Architectural. | Do. | |
| 376 | Shiyali .. | Vaithisvarankoil. | Vaithinathasvami temple .. | Archæological. | Do. | |

2-A

| Serial number. | Taluk. | Village. | Name of monument. | Reason for conservation. | Government or private; and, if latter, whether funds are available or not. | Remarks showing 'protected,' etc. |
|---|---|---|---|---|---|---|

## FIFTH CIRCLE (P.W.D.)—*cont.*

### TANJORE DISTRICT—*cont.*

| | | | | | | |
|---|---|---|---|---|---|---|
| 377 | Shiyali .. | Tirupangur. | Sivaloganathaswami temple .. | Archæological | Private (has funds). | Partly renewed. |
| 378 | Tanjore .. | Tanjore .. | Little Fort enclosing the great temple. | Historical .. | Government. | |
| 379 | Do .. | Do. .. | Great temple and inscription .. | Archæological and Architectural. | Private (has funds). | |
| 380 | Do. .. | Tillasthanam. | Gritapurisvara temple .. .. | Do. | Do. | |
| 381 | Do. .. | Perumbuliyur. | Vijagarapurisvara temple .. | Do. | Do. | |
| 382 | Do. .. | Tiruvadi .. | Panchanadesvarar temple .. | Do. | Do. | |
| 383 | Tiruttaraippundi. | Kodiyakadu. | Mantapam and inscribed stone . | Historical .. | Do. | |
| 384 | Do. .. | Kovilur .. | Siva temple .. .. .. | Archæological. | Private. | |
| 385 | Do. .. | Vedaranyam. | Do .. .. .. | Do. .. | Private (has funds). | |
| 386 | Pattukkóttai. | Avadayarkoil. | Large Siva temple .. | Archæological and Architectural. | Do. | |
| 387 | Do. .. | Arantángi. | Fort .. .. .. | Historical .. | Government. | |
| 388 | Do. .. | Pattukkóttai. | *Miniature fort and memorial column erected by the Mahratta Raja of Tanjore.* | Do. .. | Do. | |
| 389 | Do. .. | Satutavachatram. | *Ruined fort and memorial column at Saluvanayakunpatnam.* | Do. .. | Do. | |

## SIXTH CIRCLE (P.W.D.).

### MADURA DISTRICT.

| | | | | | | |
|---|---|---|---|---|---|---|
| 390 | Madura .. | Anaiyur .. | Temple .. .. .. | Archæological. | Private. | |
| 391 | Do. .. | Kodimangalam. | Subramaniaswami temple and the ruined Siva temple. | Architectural and Archæological. | Private (has funds). | |
| 392 | Do. .. | Madura .. | Meenatchi Amman temple .. | Archæological. | Do. | |
| 393 | Do. .. | Do. .. | Tirumal Naick's palace .. .. | Architectural. | Government. | |
| 394 | Do. .. | Do. .. | Teppakulam .. .. .. | Architectural and Archæological. | Private (has funds). | |
| 395 | Do. .. | Do. .. | Ten pillars .. .. | Historical .. | Government. | |
| 396 | Do. .. | Mullipallam. | Siva temple .. .. | Archæological and Architectural. | Private (no funds). | Partly renewed. |
| 397 | Do. .. | Tirupparankundram. | Remains on the hill including the rock-cut cave and inscription. | Archæological. | Private (has funds). | Protected. |
| 398 | Do. .. | Do. | Cavern with Panchapandava beds on the western slope of the hills and similar beds behind the Sikander mosque on the top. | Historical .. | Do. | |
| 399 | Do. .. | Yanamalai. | Jain cave inscription and other remains. | Archæological. | Do. | |
| 400 | Do. .. | Do. | Narasimhaswami temple with sculptures and inscriptions on a rock. | Archæological and Architectural. | Do. | |
| 401 | Mélúr . | Koilpatti .. | Temple .. .. .. | Archæological. | Government. | |
| 402 | Dindigul .. | Dindigul .. | Fort on rock .. .. | Historical .. | Do. | |
| 403 | Do. .. | Mettupatty. | Mettupatty cave in Sitharmalai .. | Archæological. | .... | |
| 404 | Mélúr .. | Alagarkovil. | Alagarmalai cavern with Panchapandava beds (midway between Alagarmalai and Kidaripatti). | Do. | Government. | |
| 405 | Do. .. | Do. | Fort .. .. .. | Historical .. | Do. | |

18

| Serial number | Taluk. | Village. | Name of monument. | Reason for conservation. | Government or private; and, if latter, whether funds are available or not. | Remarks showing 'protected,' etc. |
|---|---|---|---|---|---|---|

### SIXTH CIRCLE (P.W.D.)—cont.

#### MADURA DISTRICT—cont.

| Serial number | Taluk. | Village. | Name of monument. | Reason for conservation. | Government or private. | Remarks. |
|---|---|---|---|---|---|---|
| 406 | Mûlûr | Alagarkovil. | Temple with two tanks on the hill. | Archæological. | Private (has funds). |  |
| 407 | Do. | Do. | Tirumal Naick's palace | Architectural and Archæological. | Government. |  |
| 408 | Palni | Ettur | Rock inscription named Pandoparai. | Archæological. | .... |  |
| 409 | Do. | Ivaraimalai | Temple on hill, cave and sculptures | Do. | .... |  |
| 410 | Do. | Kiranur | Siva temple and inscriptions | Archæological and Historical. | .... |  |
| 411 | Do. | Palni | Temple on hill | Historical | Private (has funds). |  |
| 412 | Do. | Periakottai | Two old Siva temples with inscriptions. | Archæological and Historical. | .... |  |
| 413 | Tirumangalam. | Kuppalanattam. | Jain sculptures on the hillock | Archæological and Architectural. | .... |  |
| 414 | Do. | Sindupatty. | Temple | Do. | Private (has funds). |  |
| 415 | Do. | Vikramangalam. | Do. | Archæological. | Government. |  |

#### RAMNAD DISTRICT.

| 416 | Ramnad | Rámésvaram. | Tanjore Maharaja's chatram | Architectural.. | Private (has funds). |  |
| 417 | Do. | Do. | Ramanadasvami temple | Do. | Private | Partly renewed. |
| 418 | Do. | Do. | Two-storeyed mantapam | Do. | Private (has funds). |  |
| 419 | Do. | Do. | Sethumuthu Ramalinga temple | Archæological. | Do. |  |
| 420 | Do. | Devipatnam. | Jagannatha temple | Do. | Do. |  |
| 421 | Do. | Do. | Tilakesvara temple | Do. | Do. |  |
| 422 | Do. | Ramnad | Colossal figures of a horse and elephant. | Archæological and Architectural. | Do. |  |
| 423 | Sáttúr | Valliyur | Subramaniasvami temple | Do. | Do. |  |
| 424 | Srivillipattúr. | Srivillipattúr. | Tirumal Naick's palace | Do. | Government | Protected. |
| 425 | Do. | Do. | Andal temple | Archæological. | Private (has funds). |  |

#### TINNEVELLY DISTRICT.

| 426 | Nánguneri | Eruvadi | Tiruvaladesvara temple | Archæological. | Private (has funds). |  |
| 427 | Do. | Kottaikkarankulam. | Rajasimhesvara temple | Do. | Private (no funds). |  |
| 428 | Do. | Kalakkadu. | Satyavagesvara temple | Do. | Do. |  |
| 429 | Do. | Nánguneri | Vishnu temple | Do. | Do. |  |
| 430 | Do. | Padmanéri. | Nelliappasvami temple | Do. | Do. |  |
| 431 | Do. | Rathapuram. | Varaganapadhisvara temple | Do. | Private (has funds). |  |
| 432 | Do. | Shenbagaramanallur. | Jagannadhasvami temple | Do. | Private (no funds). |  |
| 433 | Do. | Tirukarankudi. | Vishnu temple | Do. | Private (has funds). |  |
| 434 | Do | Vijaya Narayanam. | Alagyamannar temple | Do. | Private (no funds). |  |
| 435 | Ottappidáram. | Kadambur. | Pre-historic burial ground | Do. | Government. |  |

14

| Serial number | Taluk. | Village. | Name of monument. | Reason for conservation. | Government or private; and, if latter, whether funds are available or not. | Remarks showing 'protected,' etc. |
|---|---|---|---|---|---|---|

## SIXTH CIRCLE (P.W.D.)—cont.

### TINNEVELLY DISTRICT—cont.

| Serial | Taluk | Village | Name of monument | Reason | Govt/Private | Remarks |
|---|---|---|---|---|---|---|
| 436 | Ottappidáram | Kalugu-malai. | Rock-cut temple on the hill | Archæological. | Zamindari (has funds). | |
| 437 | Do. | Do. | Group of Jain figures on the hill. | .... | Do. | |
| 438 | Do. | Do. | Kalugachalamurti temple | Archæological. | Private (has funds). | |
| 439 | Do. | Tuticorin | Dutch cemetery | Historical | Government. | |
| 440 | Do. | Agaram | Vishnu temple | Archæological.. | Private. | |
| 441 | Do. | Panahain-Áuruchi, | Ruined fort | Historical | Zamindari. | |
| 442 | Sankaranayi-nárkóyil. | Sankara-nayinár-kóyil. | Sankaranarayanasvami temple | Archæological. | Private (has funds). | |
| 443 | Do. | Virasika-mani. | Rock-cut caves and carvings | Do. | Do. | |
| 444 | Srívaikun-tam. | Adicha-nallur. | Pre-historic remains | Do. | Government. | |
| 445 | Do. | Alwar Tiru-nagari. | Vishnu temple | Do. | Private. | |
| 446 | Do. | Tiruchendúr. | Valliamman cave with rock-cut sculptures. | Archæological and Historical. | Private (has funds). | |
| 447 | Do. | Do. | Subramaniasvami temple .. | Archæological. | Do. | |
| 448 | Do. | Srívai-kuntam. | Vaikuntapathi temple | Do. | Do. | |
| 449 | Tinnevelly .. | Karavela-mankulam. | Varadaraja Perumal temple | Do. | Do. | |
| 450 | Do. .. | Do. | Kanakasabai temple | Do. | Private (no funds). | |
| 451 | Do. .. | Krishna-puram. | Vishnu temple | Architectural.. | Do. | |
| 452 | Do. .. | Manur .. | Rajagopalasvami temple .. | Do. .. | Do. | |
| 453 | Do. .. | Tinnevelly.. | Nelliappar temple .. | Do. .. | Private (has funds). | |
| 454 | Do. .. | Kurukku-thurai. | Cave temple of Subramaniasvami. | Do. .. | Do. | |
| 455 | Quilon (Tra-vancore State.) | Anjengo .. | Fort | Historical .. | Government. | |

### TRICHINOPOLY DISTRICT.

| Serial | Taluk | Village | Name of monument | Reason | Govt/Private | Remarks |
|---|---|---|---|---|---|---|
| 456 | Kulittalai .. | Kulittalai .. | Kadambur temple.. | Archæological. | Private (has funds). | |
| 457 | Do. .. | Ratnagiri .. | Ratnesvara temple .. | Do. | Do. | |
| 458 | Do. .. | Palaya-sangadam. | Isvara temple | Architectural.. | Private (no funds). | |
| 459 | Do. .. | Sundakka-parai. | Nagendra on a rock | Do. .. | Government. | |
| 460 | Do. .. | Sivayam .. | Ratnesvara temple and the sculp-tured rock. | Do. .. | Private (has funds). | |
| 461 | Do. .. | Palayajayan-kondan. | Ancient site including Teppakulam and Siva temple. | Archæological. | Private. | |
| 462 | Do. .. | Puratukovil. | Siva temple | Historical | Do. .. | Partly renewed. |
| 463 | Musiri .. | Srinivasa-nallur. | Korangnoathan temple .. | Archæological and Archi-tectural. | Government. | |
| 464 | Do. .. | Musiri .. | Head sluice Periavoikal alias Nattuvoikal. | Archæological and Histori-cal. | Do. | |
| 465 | Do. .. | Tiruppattúr. | Aiyanar and Kailasanatha temple. | Architectural.. | Private. | |

| Serial number. | Taluk. | Village. | Name of monument. | Reason for conservation. | Government or private ; and, if latter whether funds are available or not. | Remarks showing 'protected,' etc. |
|---|---|---|---|---|---|---|

| Serial number. | Taluk. | Village. | Name of monument. | Reason for conservation. | Government or private. | Remarks. |
|---|---|---|---|---|---|---|
| 466 | Perambalúr. | Ranjangudi attached to Tevaiyur. | Ranjangudi fort .. .. .. | Archæological. | Private .. | Protected. |
| 467 | Do. | Valikonda-puram. | Mantapam containing tombs, Shamaskhan mosque. | Do. | Government. | |
| 468 | Do. | Do. | Temple, tank and mantapam .. | Do. | Private (no funds). | Protected. |
| 469 | Do. | Vallapuram, hamlet of Brama-desam. | Mantapam containing a tomb .. | Do. | Do. | Do. |
| 470 | Do. | Do. | Shamaskhan mosque .. .. | Do. | Do. | Do. |
| 471 | Do. | Arumbavur. | Siva temple .. .. .. | Do. | Private. | |
| 472 | Do. | Aduthorai .. | Do. .. .. .. | Do. | Do. | |
| 473 | Do. | Ullathur .. | Do. .. .. .. | Do. | Do. | |
| 474 | Trichinopoly. | Bikshandar-kovil. | Tirumurthisvami temple .. | Do. | Private (has funds) | |
| 475 | Do. | Kilapaluvur. | Siva temple with inscriptions .. | Archæological and Historical. | Private (no funds). | |
| 476 | Do. | Konaaalem. | Venkatesvara Perumal temple .. | Do. | Do. | |
| 477 | Do. | Lalgudi .. | Siva temple .. .. .. | Architectural .. | Do. | |
| 478 | Do. | Trichinopoly. | Fort with temple and inscriptions. | Do. .. | Government. | |
| 479 | Do. | Do. | Nathad Shah's mosque .. .. | Do .. | Private (has funds). | |
| 480 | Do. | Do. | Nawab's palace .. .. | Do. .. | Private. | |
| 481 | Do. | Do. | Two rock-cut caves on Trichino-poly rock. | Do. .. | Private (has funds). | Protected. |
| 482 | Do. | Do. | Thayumanasvami temple .. | Archæological. | Do. | |
| 483 | Do. | Tiruppala-thurai. | Siva temple .. .. | Do. | Do. | Partly renewed. |
| 484 | Do. | Tiruvaram-bur. | Erumbesvara temple .. .. | Do. | Do. | |
| 485 | Do. | Tiruvellarai. | Jambunatham temple and rock inscriptions. | Do. | Private (no funds). | |
| 486 | Do. | Do. | Pundarikaksha Perumal temple with well on the south-west of it. | Do. | Do. | |
| 487 | Do. | Tiruvanak-kaval. | Small Chola temple of Raja-rajesvara, north of Jembukes-varam temple. | Do. | Do. | |
| 488 | Do. | Do. | Jambukesvara temple .. .. | Do. | Private (has funds). | Partly renewed. |
| 489 | Do. | Srirangam . | Rauganadasvami temple .. .. | Historical and Architectural. | Do. | |
| 490 | Do. | Samayapu-ram. | Rojesvarnsvami temple .. .. | Architectural. | Do. | |
| 491 | Do. | Do. | Ancient site .. .. .. | Do. | Government. | |
| 492 | Do. | Alambakam. | Siva temple .. .. .. | Archæological. | Private. | |
| 493 | Do. | Do. | Varadarajaperumal temple .. | Do. | Do. | |
| 494 | Do. | Samayapu-ram. | Mahakali temple .. .. | Do. | Do. | |
| 495 | Do. | Toroiyur .. | Siva temple .. .. | Do. | Do. | |
| 496 | Do. | Virapatti .. | Jain image in Annavasal.. .. | Do. | Do. | |
| 497 | Do. | Vellanur .. | Jain image .. .. .. | Do. | Do. | |
| 498 | Do | Tiruvedangu-lam. | Siva temple .. .. | Do. | Do. | |
| 499 | Do | Ratnagudi .. | Inscriptions on Anicut .. .. | Historical .. | Do. | |
| 500 | Do. | Uyakondan Tirumalai. | Temple and Cholamparai Rock with inscriptions. | Archæological and Historical. | Private (has funds). | |

| Serial number. | Taluk. | Village. | Name of monument. | Reason for conservation. | Government or private; and, if latter, whether funds are available or not. | Remarks showing 'protected,' etc. |
|---|---|---|---|---|---|---|

## SIXTH CIRCLE (P.W.D.)—cont.

### TRICHINOPOLY DISTRICT—cont.

| Serial number. | Taluk. | Village. | Name of monument. | Reason for conservation. | Government or private. | Remarks |
|---|---|---|---|---|---|---|
| 501 | Udaiyár-pálaiyam. | Gangai-koudashola-puram. | Brihadisvarasvami temple .. | Historical and Architectural. | Private (no funds). | * |
| 502 | Do. | Near Gan-gaikonda-sholapuram. | Kuruvelappankovil .. | Archæological. | Private. | |
| 503 | Do. | Jayankonda-sólapuram. | Jain statues .. .. | Architectural. | Do. .. | Protected. |
| 504 | Do. | Kamaraea-valli. | Siva temple .. .. | Archæological. | Private (no funds). | |
| 505 | Do. | Tirumala-vadi. | Temple .. .. .. .. | Historical .. | Private (has funds). | |

# APPENDIX A.

### THE ANCIENT MONUMENTS PRESERVATION ACT (VII OF '1904).

*An Act to provide for the preservation of Ancient Monuments and of objects of archæological, historical or artistic interest.*

WHEREAS it is expedient to provide for the preservation of ancient monuments, for the exercise of control over traffic in antiquities and over excavation in certain places, and for the protection and acquisition in certain cases of ancient monuments and of objects of archæological, historical or artistic interest; It is hereby enacted as follows:—

Short title and extent. 1. (*1*) This Act may be called the Ancient Monuments Preservation Act, 1904.

(*2*) It extends to the whole of British India, inclusive of British Baluchistan, the Sonthal Parganas and the Pargana of Spiti.

Definitions. 2. In this Act, unless there is anything repugnant in the subject or context,—

(*1*) "ancient monument" means any structure, erection or monument, or any tumulus or place of interment, or any cave, rock-sculpture, inscription or monolith which is of historical, archæological or artistic interest, or any remains thereof, and includes—

    (*a*) the site of an ancient monument:

    (*b*) such portion of land adjoining the site of an ancient monument as may be required for fencing or covering in or otherwise preserving such monument; and

    (*c*) the means of access to and convenient inspection of an ancient monument:

(*2*) "antiquities" include any moveable objects which the Government, by reason of their historical or archæological associations, may think it necessary to protect against injury, removal or dispersion:

(*3*) "Commissioner" includes any officer authorized by the Local Government to perform the duties of a Commissioner under this Act:

(*4*) "maintain" and "maintenance" include the fencing, covering in, repairing, restoring and cleansing of a protected monument, and the doing of any act which may be necessary for the purpose of maintaining a protected monument or of securing convenient access thereto:

(*5*) "land" includes a revenue-free estate, a revenue-paying estate, and a permanent transferable tenure, whether such estate or tenure be subject to incumbrances or not: and

(*6*) "owner" includes a joint owner invested with powers of management on behalf of himself and other joint owners, and any manager or trustee exercising powers of management over an ancient monument, and the successor in title of any such owner and the successor in office of any such manager or trustee.

Provided that nothing in this Act shall be deemed to extend the powers which may lawfully be exercised by such manager or trustee.

Protected monuments. 3. (*1*) The Local Government may, by notification in the local official Gazette, declare an ancient monument to be a protected monument within the meaning of this Act.

(*2*) A copy of every notification published under sub-section (1) shall be fixed up in a conspicuous place on or near the monument, together with an intimation that any objections to the issue of the notification received by the Local Government within one month from the date when it is so fixed up will be taken into consideration.

(*3*) On the expiry of the said period of one month, the Local Government, after considering the objections, if any, shall confirm or withdraw the notification.

(*4*) A notification published under this section shall, unless and until it is withdrawn, be conclusive evidence of the fact that the monument to which it relates is an ancient monument within the meaning of this Act.

### *Ancient Monuments.*

Acquisition of rights in or guardianship of an ancient monument. 4. (*1*) The Collector, with the sanction of the Local Government, may purchase or take a lease of any protected monument.

(*2*) The Collector, with the like sanction, may accept a gift or bequest of any protected monument.

(3) The owner of any protected monument may, by written instrument, constitute the Commissioner the guardian of the monument, and the Commissioner may, with the sanction of the Local Government, accept such guardianship.

(4) When the Commissioner has accepted the guardianship of a monument under subsection (3), the owner shall, except as expressly provided in this Act, have the same estate, right, title and interest in and to the monument as if the Commissioner had not been constituted guardian thereof.

(5) When the Commissioner has accepted the guardianship of a monument under subsection (3), the provisions of this Act relating to agreements executed under section 5 shall apply to the written instrument executed under the said sub-section.

(6) Where a protected monument is without an owner, the Commissioner may assume the guardianship of the monument.

5. (1) The Collector may, with the previous sanction of the Local Government, propose to the owner to enter into an agreement with the Secretary of State for India in Council for the preservation of any protected monument in his district.

*Preservation of ancient monument by agreement.*

(2) An agreement under this section may provide for the following matters, or for such of them as it may be found expedient to include in the agreement :—

   (a) the maintenance of the monument ;

   (b) the custody of the monument, and the duties of any person who may be employed to watch it ;

   (c) the restriction of the owner's right to destroy, remove, alter or deface the monument or to build on or near the site of the monument ;

   (d) the facilities of access to be permitted to the public or to any portion of the public and to persons deputed by the owner or the Collector to inspect or maintain the monument ;

   (e) the notice to be given to the Government in case the land on which the monument is situated is offered for sale by the owner, and the right to be reserved to the Government to purchase such land, or any specified portion of such land, at its market value ;

   (f) the payment of any expenses incurred by the owner or by the Government in connection with the preservation of the monument ;

   (g) the proprietary or other rights which are to rest in His Majesty in respect of the monument when any expenses are incurred by the Government in connection with the preservation of the monument ;

   (h) the appointment of an authority to decide any dispute arising out of the agreement ; and

   (i) any matter connected with the preservation of the monument which is a proper subject of agreement between the owner and the Government.

(3) An agreement under this section may be executed by the Collector on behalf of the Secretary of State for India in Council, but shall not be so executed until it has been approved by the Local Government.

(4) The terms of an agreement under this section may be altered from time to time with the sanction of the Local Government and with the consent of the owner.

(5) With the previous sanction of the Local Government, the Collector may terminate an agreement under this section on giving six months' notice in writing to the owner.

(6) The owner may terminate an agreement under this section on giving six months' notice to the Collector.

(7) An agreement under this section shall be binding on any person claiming to be owner of the monument to which it relates, through or under a party by whom or on whose behalf the agreement was executed.

(8) Any rights acquired by Government in respect of expenses incurred in protecting or preserving a monument shall not be affected by the termination of an agreement under this section.

6. (1) If the owner is unable, by reason of infancy or other disability, to act for himself, the person legally competent to act on his behalf may exercise the powers conferred upon an owner by section 5.

*Owners under disability or not in possession.*

(2) In the case of village property, the headman or other village-officer exercising powers of management over such property may exercise the powers conferred upon an owner by section 5.

(3) Nothing in this section shall be deemed to empower any person not being of the same religion as the persons on whose behalf he is acting to make or execute an agreement relating to a protected monument which or any part of which is periodically used for the religious worship or observances of that religion.

7. (1) If the Collector apprehends that the owner or occupier of a monument intends to destroy, remove, alter, deface, or imperil the monument or to build on or near the site thereof in contravention of the terms of an agreement for its preservation under section 5, the Collector may make an order prohibiting any such contravention of the agreement.

*Enforcement of agreement.*

(2) If an owner or other person who is bound by an agreement for the preservation or maintenance of a monument under section 5 refuses to do any act which is in the opinion of the Collector necessary to such preservation or maintenance, or neglects to do any such act within such reasonable time as may be fixed by the Collector, the Collector may authorise any person to do any such act, and the expense of doing any such act or such portion of the expense as the owner may be liable to pay under the agreement may be recovered from the owner as if it were an arrear of land-revenue.

(3) A person aggrieved by an order made under this section may appeal to the Commissioner, who may cancel or modify it and whose decision shall be final.

8. Every person who purchases, at a sale for arrears of land-revenue or any other public demand, or at a sale made under the Bengal Patni Taluks Regulation, 1819, an estate or tenure in which is situated a monument in respect of which any instrument has been executed by the owner for the time being, under section 4 or section 5, and every person claiming any title to a monument from, through or under an owner who executed any such instrument, shall be bound by such instrument.

*II of 1819.* Purchasers at certain sales and persons claiming through owner bound by instrument executed by owner.

9. (1) If any owner or other person competent to enter into an agreement under section 5 for the preservation of a protected monument, refuses or fails to enter into such an agreement when proposed to him by the Collector, and if any endowment has been created for the purpose of keeping such monument in repair, or for that purpose among others, the Collector may institute a suit in the Court of the District Judge, or, if the estimated cost of repairing the monument does not exceed one thousand rupees, may make an application to the District Judge for the proper application of such endowment or part thereof.

Application of endowment to repair an ancient monument.

(2) On the hearing of an application under sub-section (1), the District Judge may summon and examine the owner and any person whose evidence appears to him necessary, and may pass an order for the proper application of the endowment or of any part thereof, and any such order may be executed as if it were the decree of a Civil Court.

10. (1) If the Local Government apprehends that a protected monument is in danger of being destroyed, injured, or allowed to fall into decay, the Local Government may proceed to acquire it under the provisions of the Land Acquisition Act, 1894, as if the preservation of a protected monument were a "public purpose" within the meaning of that Act.

Compulsory purchase of ancient monument.

*of 1894.*

(2) The powers of compulsory purchase conferred by sub-section (1) shall not be exercised in the case of—

(a) any monument which or any part of which is periodically used for religious observances ; or

(b) any monument which is the subject of a subsisting agreement executed under section 5.

(3) In any case other than the cases referred to in sub-section (2) the said powers of compulsory purchase shall not be exercised unless the owner or other person competent to enter into an agreement under section 5 has failed, within such reasonable period as the Collector may fix in this behalf, to enter into an agreement proposed to him under the said section or has terminated or given notice of his intention to terminate such an agreement.

11. (1) The Commissioner shall maintain every monument in respect of which the Government has acquired any of the rights mentioned in section 4 or which the Government has acquired under section 10.

Maintenance of certain protected monuments.

(2) When the Commissioner has accepted the guardianship of a monument under section 4, he shall, for the purpose of maintaining such monument, have access to the monument at all reasonable times, by himself and by his agents, subordinates and workmen, for the purpose of inspecting the monument, and for the purpose of bringing such materials and doing such acts as he may consider necessary or desirable for the maintenance thereof.

12. The Commissioner may receive voluntary contributions towards the cost of maintaining a protected monument and may give orders as to the management and application of any funds so received by him:

Voluntary contributions.

Provided that no contribution received under this section shall be applied to any purpose other than the purpose for which it was contributed.

13. (1) A place of worship or shrine maintained by the Government under this Act shall not be used for any purpose inconsistent with its character.

Protection of place of worship from misuse, pollution or desecration.

(2) Where the Collector has, under section 4, purchased or taken a lease of any protected monument, or has accepted a gift or bequest, or the Commissioner has, under the same section, accepted the guardianship thereof, and such monument, or any part thereof, is periodically used for religious worship or observances by any community, the Collector shall make due provision for the protection of such monument, or such part thereof, from pollution or desecration —

(a) by prohibiting the entry therein, except in accordance with conditions prescribed with the concurrence of the persons in religious charge of the said monument or part thereof, of any person not entitled so to enter by the religious usages of the community by which the monument or part thereof is used, or

(b) by taking such other action as he may think necessary in this behalf.

**Relinquishment of Government rights in a monument.** 14. With the sanction of the Local Government, the Commissioner may—

(*a*) where rights have been acquired by Government in respect of any monument under this Act by virtue of any sale, lease, gift or will, relinquish the rights so acquired to the person who would for the time being be the owner of the monument if such rights had not been acquired ; or

(*b*) relinquish any guardianship of a monument which he has accepted under this Act.

**Right of access to certain protected monuments.** 15. (*1*) Subject to such rules as may after previous publication be made by the Local Government, the public shall have a right of access to any monument maintained by the Government under this Act.

(*2*) In making any rule under sub-section (*1*), the Local Government may provide that a breach of it shall be punishable with fine which may extend to twenty rupees.

**Penalties.** 16. Any person other than the owner who destroys, removes, injures, alters, defaces or imperils a protected monument, and any owner who destroys, removes, injures, alters, defaces or imperils a monument maintained by Government under this Act or in respect of which an agreement has been executed under section 5, and any owner or occupier who contravenes an order made under section 7, sub-section (1), shall be punishable with fine which may extend to five thousand rupees, or with imprisonment which may extend to three months, or with both.

### *Traffic in Antiquities.*

**Power to Governor General in Council to control traffic in antiquities.** 17. (*1*) If the Governor General in Council apprehends that antiquities are being sold or removed to the detriment of India or of any neighbouring country, he may, by notification in the *Gazette of India*, prohibit or restrict the bringing or taking by sea or by land of any antiquities or class of antiquities described in the notification into or out of British India or any specified part of British India.

(*2*) Any person who brings or takes or attempts to bring or take any such antiquities into or out of British India or any part of British India in contravention of a notification issued under sub-section (*1*), shall be punishable with fine which may extend to five hundred rupees.

(*3*) Antiquities in respect of which an offence referred to in sub-section (*2*) has been committed shall be liable to confiscation.

(*4*) An officer of customs, or an officer of Police of a grade not lower than Sub-Inspector, duly empowered by the Local Government in this behalf, may search any vessel, cart or other means of conveyance, and may open any baggage or package of goods, if he has reason to believe that goods in respect of which an offence has been committed under sub-section (*2*) are contained therein.

(*5*) A person who complains that the power of search mentioned in sub-section (*4*) has been vexatiously or improperly exercised may address his complaint to the Local Government, and the Local Government shall pass such order and may award such compensation, if any, as appears to it to be just.

### *Protection of Sculptures, Carvings, Images, Bas-reliefs, Inscriptions or like objects.*

**Power to Local Government to control moving of sculptures, carvings or like objects.** 18. (*1*) If the Local Government considers that any sculptures, carvings, images, bas-reliefs, inscriptions or other like objects ought not to be moved from the place where they are without the sanction of the Government, the Local Government may, by notification in the local official Gazette, direct that any such object or any class of such object shall not be moved unless with the written permission of the Collector.

(*2*) A person applying for the permission mentioned in sub-section (*1*) shall specify the object or objects which he proposes to move, and shall furnish, in regard to such object or objects, any information which the Collector may require.

(*3*) If the Collector refuses to grant such permission, the applicant may appeal to the Commissioner, whose decision shall be final.

(*4*) Any person who moves any object in contravention of a notification issued under sub-section (1), shall be punishable with fine which may extend to five hundred rupees.

(*5*) If the owner of any property proves to the satisfaction of the Local Government that he has suffered any loss or damage by reason of the inclusion of such property in a notification published under sub-section (*1*), the Local Government shall either

(*a*) exempt such property from the said notification ;

(*b*) purchase such property, if it be moveable, at its market-value ; or

(*c*) pay compensation for any loss or damage sustained by the owner of such property, if it be immoveable.

**Purchase of sculptures, carvings or like objects by the Government.** 19. (*1*) If the Local Government apprehends that any object mentioned in a notification issued under section 18, sub-section (*1*), is in danger of being destroyed, removed, injured or allowed to fall into decay, the Local Government may pass orders for the compulsory purchase of such object at its market-value, and the Collector shall thereupon give notice to the owner of the object to be purchased.

(2) The power of compulsory purchase given by this section shall not extend to—
    (a) any image or symbol actually used for the purpose of any religious observance; or
    (b) anything which the owner desires to retain on any reasonable ground personal to himself or to any of his ancestors or to any member of his family.

### Excavations.

20. (1) If the Local Government is of opinion that excavation within the limits of any local area ought to be restricted or regulated for the purpose of protecting or preserving any ancient monument, the Local Government may, by notification in the local official Gazette, make rules—
    (a) fixing the boundaries of the area to which the rules are to apply; and
    (b) prescribing the authority by which, and the terms on which, licenses to excavate may be granted.

*Power to Local Government to control excavation.*

(2) The power to make rules given by this section is subject to the condition of rules being made after previous publication.

(3) A rule made under this section may provide that any person committing a breach thereof shall be punishable with fine which may extend to two hundred rupees.

(4) If any owner or occupier of land included in a notification under sub-section (1), proves to the satisfaction of the Local Government that he has sustained any loss by reason of such land being so included, the Local Government shall pay compensation in respect of such loss.

### General.

21. (1) The market-value of any property which Government is empowered to purchase at such value under this Act, or the amount of compensation to be paid by Government in respect of anything done under this Act, shall, where any dispute arises touching the amount of such market-value or compensation, be ascertained in the manner provided by the Land Acquisition Act, 1894, sections 3, 8 to 34, 45 to 47, 51 and 52, so far as they can be made applicable:

*Assessment of market-value or compensation.*

*I of 1894.*

Provided that when making an inquiry under the said Land Acquisition Act, 1894, the Collector shall be assisted by two assessors, one of whom shall be a competent person nominated by the Collector, and one a person nominated by the owner or, in case the owner fails to nominate an assessor within such reasonable time as may be fixed by the Collector in this behalf, by the Collector.

*Jurisdiction.*

22. A Magistrate of the third class shall not have jurisdiction to try any person charged with an offence against this Act.

*Power to make rules.*

23. (1) The Governor General in Council or the Local Government may make rules for carrying out any of the purposes of this Act.

(2) The power to make rules given by this section is subject to the condition of the rules being made after previous publication.

*Protection to public servants acting under Act.*

24. No suit for compensation and no criminal proceeding shall lie against any public servant in respect of any act done, or in good faith intended to be done, in the exercise of any power conferred by this Act.

# APPENDIX B.

### *GENERAL PRINCIPLES FOR THE GUIDANCE OF THOSE ENTRUSTED WITH THE CUSTODY OF, AND EXECUTION OF REPAIRS TO, ANCIENT MONUMENTS.

The chief aim of conservation should be to preserve and perpetuate authentic specimens of the monumental antiquities of the country rather than to rebuild or renew them; and not so much to add new work in imitation of what the original is thought to have been, as to preserve what is left of it. It may be laid down, as a first principle, that, as funds will necessarily be limited, they should be economised in such a way as to preserve, as far as is practicable, as many of the most important ancient works as possible; and, to this end, preservation should be primarily aimed at, and repair attempted only in cases where its advisability is undoubted, and where special funds can be provided for the purpose. Of the buildings deserving repair only a very limited number can be restored in the course of the year, and many will have to wait, it may be, five, or ten, or fifteen years before they can be taken thoroughly in hand; but each year the annual work of protecting and conserving them all must go on with unbroken regularity, so that when the time comes for repairing them, it may not be found that neglect, in the meantime, has necessitated a much greater outlay than would otherwise have been incurred.

*The selection of monuments.*—As regards the selection of monuments for conservation, it is difficult, if not impossible, to lay down any comprehensive principles which can be applied to each and every case. First, there are the individual merits of the monument to be weighed; its historic importance; its architectural value; or any features which it may possess of peculiar interest for the religious or artistic history of the country. Then its comparative merits in relation to other monuments in its immediate vicinity must be taken into account; for, in some localities, where there is a dearth of first class monuments, it may well be worth conserving a second rate building, which elsewhere would be allowed to fall to ruin. A variety of particular considerations of this kind defy the application of principles broad enough to embrace them all.

The selection of monuments for conservation and the extent and manner of carrying out their repairs, are matters requiring the advice of the local Archæological Officer. He will, of course, gladly avail himself of any helpful opinions in these matters, but it must be understood that he alone is responsible to Government, and his attention should be called to every case of proposed conservation upon whatever scale it may be.

*Estimates.*—Every estimate for work should be submitted to the Archæological Officer, in the first instance, for his approval and signature, and care should be taken that nothing be subsequently added to or omitted from it without consulting him.

*Classification.*—The following classification of monuments has been laid down by the Government of India, and they are so classified in the margins of the different lists of Antiquarian Remains issued by the Archæological Department, as well as in the various progress reports.

    I.—Those monuments which from their present condition or historical or archæological value ought to be maintained in permanent good repair.

    II.—Those monuments which it is now only possible or desirable to save from further decay by such minor measures as the eradication of vegetation, the exclusion of water from the walls, and the like.

    III.—Those monuments which, from their advanced stage of decay or comparative unimportance, it is impossible or unnecessary to preserve.

The monuments in classes I and II are further sub-divided thus—

    I (*a*) and II (*a*).—Monuments in the possession or charge of Government, or in respect of which Government must undertake the cost of all measures of conservation.

    I (*b*) and II (*b*).—Monuments in the possession or charge of private bodies or individuals.

No comment is necessary upon class I. But in class II it will often be found necessary to carry out sufficient initial repairs, over and above those specified, to put a building in such a state that those minor measures will afterwards suffice to keep it in a tolerably fair condition.

Because a building is put into class III, on account of its very dilapidated condition, it does not follow that there should be any unseemly haste in converting it into road metal: it may still be a monument of interest as long as it keeps together.

*Preliminary measures.*—The first thing to be done, after the selection of a building for conservation, and before laying hands upon it at all, is to ascertain how it stands with respect to the provisions of the Ancient Monuments Preservation Act. If already in Government possession it will, or should be, in the custody of the local Public Works Department for repairs, and should be upon their lists as a Protected Monument. If not, the chief civil authority in the

---

* This was issued by Mr. J. H. Marshall, Director-General of Archæology.

district should be asked to deal with it under the Act, in the manner considered most desirable. Such preliminary precautions will save friction with owners at the time of carrying out repairs. This should be followed by the acquisition of ground around the monument, if necessary, by fencing, and by the appointment of caretakers when advisable. In places frequented by visitors, likely to scribble their names and commit other nuisances, notice boards may be necessary. These, while being conspicuous enough to attract attention, should not be such as to be an eyesore; nor should they disfigure the monument by being set up upon the face of it or directly in front of it. The narrowest part of the approach to the precincts is, in most cases, the best place for their erection.

*Preservation before repair.*—Officers charged with the execution of conservation work should never forget that the reparation of any remnant of ancient architecture, however humble, is a work to be entered upon with totally different feelings from a new work or from the repairs of a modern building. Although there are many ancient buildings, whose state of disrepair suggests at first sight a renewal, it should never be forgotten that their historical value is gone when their authenticity is destroyed, and that our first duty is not to renew them but to preserve them. When, therefore, repairs are carried out, no effort should be spared to save as many parts of the original as possible, since it is to the authenticity of the old parts that practically all the interest attaching to the new will owe itself.

*Supervision.*—The success of conservation depends upon the degree of personal supervision given by the Engineer in charge and the Archæological officer as much as upon the skill of the workmen employed. The unusual and peculiar treatment that work on oriental structures demands, calls for the full attention and thought of the Executive Officer in charge; it is, as a rule, beyond the ability and intelligence of the lower subordinates, to whom the work is, too often, entirely relegated.

Native artizans are usually good copyists, capable of imitating any model which may be set before them, but unable to make use of their eyes, and being accustomed to work with a stereotyped series of degenerate modern imitations, they apply them indiscriminately, in place and out of it, on all classes of buildings. And many otherwise good workmen are prone to show off their skill by trying to improve upon the original. This tendency has to be carefully guarded against.

*Vegetation.*—One of the principal factors in causing the ruin of brick and stone buildings is the growth of vegetation in the joints, and the only way of dealing with this evil is constantly to eradicate the plants before they have the chance of becoming firmly rooted. For this purpose, inspections of every building should be made by the engineer in charge at least once in the year.

A mixture called "Scrub Eradicator," manufactured by Messrs. Fleming & Co. of Bombay, is recommended for the removal and prevention of weeds. It can be applied with safety to any building material, whether marble, sandstone or mortar.

*Removal of masonry, etc.*—It is not generally desirable to demolish or remove, in whole or in part, any stone or brickwork which it is at all possible to repair *in situ.* If new work has to be inserted, any mouldings or other details, which may have to be worked on it, should be in strict harmony with the adjoining ornaments. In removing broken or decayed work do not take out any but such as is so far gone as to have lost all its original form; better to have broken or half decayed original work than the smartest and most perfect new work.

With regard to walls out of plumb, it is not always necessary to dismantle and rebuild them. In many cases it will be found that the fault was caused soon after the erection of the building by the subsidence of the foundations, which, having permanently settled, are not likely to go any further. If there is any suspicion of movement, the wall or walls may be watched from time to time and any movement noted.

When dismantling masonry, previous to rebuilding, it is necessary to mark or number the old stones so as, the more readily, to replace them in their original positions. In doing this, care should be taken not to use oil paint, or other pigment or stain, that it will be difficult to remove again. It is better to put the numbers on the sides or back of the stone rather than upon the face. In any case, all marks should be removed on completion of the work.

*Replacement of missing architectural details.*—Should it be necessary, at any time, to replace any architectural detail which has disappeared, examination should be made of any similar feature in another part of the building itself, or on one of similar style in the neighbourhood. In restorations of this kind the assistance of the Archæological Department should invariably be invoked.

In the case of ruined Hindu temples which, as a rule, have been covered with sculpture, very great help may be afforded towards any necessary rebuilding of the fallen material, where it remains *in situ,* by a careful survey of the *debris* before a single stone is lifted from the ground. A stone, falling from the walls or roof, will naturally come to the ground on a spot as near as possible vertically below the position it originally occupied; and so its place upon the ground will generally indicate its former position. A rough sketch plan of the temple should be made, on which the ground, immediately around the base of the building, is marked off into separate areas. The individual stones can then be marked (not on their faces) according to the area in which they lie. The position of fallen statues should be separately and carefully plotted, for they generally have their appointed niches and positions upon the walls, which may not be changed. To gather up these fallen stones, and to mix them indiscriminately, would cause hopeless confusion, in the effort of re-sorting them, to those unfamiliar with the construction of such shrines. These remarks apply, also, to the excavation of sculptures embedded in the *debris* accumulated around the bases of temples. Very great care is necessary in such cases not to damage the sculptures, or the basement mouldings of the temple in the operation. Excavated areas, especially around buildings, should not be left as pits to collect water and so rot the masonry, but should be carefully drained.

*Effacement of traces of old designs.*—When any feature of a building is too far decayed to be restored, the spot which it occupied must not be plastered over so as to destroy all traces of its ever having been there. This should apply to all classes of architectural detail, and, even though a small fragment only remains, it ought not to be obliterated.

*New stone work.*—All the new stone work should be matched in colour with the surfaces adjoining it. It frequently happens that the same quarry yields several varieties of the same stone, and care should be taken, when putting in new patches, to procure the same variety as has been used in the contiguous masonry. In some cases, too, where the old stone work has weathered to a darker tint, it may be necessary, in order to avoid any violent or unpleasant contrast between the new and old surfaces to use artificial means for staining the former. The stain will wear off in course of time, but not until the surface has weathered to a better colour.

*Roofs and walls.*—Accumulation of soil on roofs or other flat surfaces should be removed as favouring the growth of vegetation. Any openings on terraced roofs, through which rain water can percolate, should be stopped, and proper drainage provided for. Cracks on the roof, where they are not observable, may be pointed; but on the walls, both exterior and interior, simple grouting (if that is necessary and practicable) should be employed. In this process the mortar can be prevented from coming too near the surface by first stopping the joints with clay from the outside, which can be removed when the grouting within is dry.

*Cement and pointing.*—If the new stones are accurately dressed, so as to fit closely to one another, there will generally be no necessity for mortar or any cementing material in the joints. Old stone buildings were originally erected, as a rule, entirely without mortar. If it should, in any exceptional case, be necessary, let the mortar be in great part composed of Portland cement. In no case should any mortar be seen upon the surface of the work where mortar has not been used originally. Nor should pointing, as it is generally understood in India, be permitted, on any account, either in brick or stone work, except in places where it is not exposed to view. Pointing on ancient buildings is an anachronism which cannot be too strongly guarded against. All mortar joints, in which, during previous repairs, the mortar has not been confined to the joint, but has been smeared over the adjacent stone, should be carefully scraped.

*Clamps and dowels.*—Clamps and dowels may be used to strengthen stone work, but they must be of copper or gun-metal, and not of iron, as the latter metal will oxidize and split the stoutest masonry. It may be added here that, if iron or steel is used for supports or other purposes, it should not be brought into direct contact with the stone, but should be protected with a coating of cement, or a casing of some other suitable material.

*Broken lintels, etc.*—As a rule broken lintels or beams may be supported by skilfully stirruping them up from above, or, if that is impracticable, by inserting angle iron beneath; but in cases where a pier, not forming part of the original design, has to be introduced, it should be made quite apparent that it is a later addition, without, however, rendering it obtrusive by pointing or by other purely modern devices.

One of the most commonly occurring repairs in buildings, constructed on the pillar and lintel style, is that of broken beams or lintels. It is seldom necessary to remove a broken beam in order to substitute a whole one—a work generally accompanied with considerable difficulty. Angle iron, running along the two bottom edges of a beam, the latter being carried into the angle of the flanges, with the ends let in, for support, between the soffit of the beam and the top of the bracket-capital, has been used with great success. The angle iron can be used angle up or angle down. This, and a variety of other methods, will be found described and illustrated with diagrams in the Progress Report of the Archæological Survey, Western Circle, for the year 1905-1906.

*Brickwork.*—In repairing brickwork, bricks of the same size as the original should be used; they can frequently be obtained without any difficulty, at a minimum cost, from old dismantled buildings. The mortar joints, also, should be of the same thickness as in the old work; and if the adjoining surface of the brickwork, which is not to be repaired, is much decayed, the mortar joints of the new work may be recessed about ¼″ to ½″, so as to avoid the appearance of great newness.

On sites like that of Pagan in Burma, where there are vast quantities of old bricks, close at hand, for the workmen to use, where much of the brickwork is without mortar, and where the cost of repair means little more than the cost of the labour employed, we need not hesitate to repair any prominent features, such as battlements, cornices, and the like, the absence of which seriously detracts from the beauty of the structure, and whose reconstruction is a perfectly straightforward matter, involving no doubts or difficulties whatever.

*Plaster stucco.*—In cases where stucco has either peeled off completely, or adheres only here and there in small patches, the renewal of the plaster facing and the destruction of whatever remnants are left of the original stucco is a blunder which, unfortunately, has only too frequently been committed. Upon wall surfaces the course to be invariably followed is to cut away, where it is necessary, just so much of the old stucco as has separated completely from the walls and to edge round the remainder with cement so as to prevent rain-water percolating behind, the brick work being pointed, if necessary, to keep out rain-water, with recessed pointing as previously

described. On no account ought the picturesque aspect of the exposed brickwork to be spoilt by covering it with new and glaring plaster or whitewash. Where only comparatively small gaps occur in *ornamental* stucco work, and its repair is consequently desirable, care should be taken to avoid the insertion of modern designs. Whenever broken parts have to be replaced, as for instance in balustrades, mouldings and the like, the existing old designs, which generally consist of one pattern repeated, or of two alternating with each other, should be faithfully copied.

This does not, however, apply to terraces, roofs, and domes, the original plaster of which must be kept in repair to keep them watertight. But in such cases there is no necessity for repairing their surfaces with raw white plaster in ugly patches and lines. A dark coloured plaster should be used so as to match, as nearly as possible, the old discoloured work. A mixture, that has been found very successful for this purpose, and which can be varied to match most discolourations, is as follows :—

|  | SEERS. |
|---|---|
| Kankar lime | 25 |
| Cement | 2½ |
| Black slag from brick kilns roughly ground | 7½ |

|  | CHITTAKS. |
|---|---|
| Black colouring matter extracted from the cooked fruit of the wild pomegranate (*Narli*) | 4 |

|  | SEERS. |
|---|---|
| Gur (Black Sugar) | 1 |
| Hemp (*Sunn*) | 1½ |

*Weather stains.*—Weather stains, upon the outside of a building, should not ordinarily be removed, but white lichens, or other small growths of that kind, should, if practicable, be cleaned away where they obscure delicate carvings beneath them ; but do not let the remedy be worse than the defect by leaving unsightly marks of the cleaning.

*Carvings, etc.*—As a rule, the repair of carvings, whether in stone or brick, should be limited to those of a purely geometric design. The repair of divine or human figures, or of free floral designs, is scarcely ever to be advocated ; nor, indeed, in reproducing some geometric designs, is it advisable to do more than indicate their main lines. Questions of such repair, however, must be decided on their own merits and always after consultation with the local archæological authority. Every scrap of ancient tilework or carved brick, that is lying in the *debris* on old sites, should be restored, if possible, to its former place, care, of course, being taken to ensure the restoration being correct.

*Images.*—An image that has fallen should never be replaced on a pedestal or in a niche unless it is absolutely certain that it was originally set there. No end of confusion may be caused by the indiscriminate re-erection of images in the wrong places.

No new images should ever be provided. Empty niches should remain empty if their images are lost, and the spaces occupied in friezes and string courses should, in repaired portions, be blank. Broken images should not be mended with new limbs or other parts, but old portions, if existing, may be pieced together as far as is practicable.

*Whitewash.*—The use of whitewash or paint, especially on sculptures and inscriptions, should be forbidden. If it is contemplated to remove any from an old surface, precautions must be taken to prevent injury to any inscription, relief or painting beneath. Whitewash may often be removed by brushing with native soap and water, or light sponging in the case of painted or delicate surfaces, but, if it will not yield to this treatment, a weak solution of nitric acid or, in cases where the action of nitric acid may be deleterious, of acetic acid, may be used, followed by a thorough washing down with water in which a little carbonate of soda has been dissolved. It has been found that kerosine-oil is effective in removing whitewash off tilework.

*Decorative tilework.*—In cases where pieces of tiles have fallen away, leaving gaps in the surface, the gaps should not be filled with plaster. The tiles next the gaps should be edged round with cement to prevent more of them from falling. The cement should on no account be coloured to imitate the tiles, but may be mixed with colouring matter, so as to approach the tint of the old cementing material.

*Wooden buildings.*—The principles applying to the conservation of wooden buildings must, owing to the nature of their material and the comparative short duration of their existence, necessarily differ from the principles applying to structures in brick or stone. Once a brick or stone structure is put into a good state of repair, we may expect that, with a little attention from time to time, it may last for several hundred years.

This is far from being the case with wooden structures, and, as a rule, the strictest economy must be observed in their conservation. In the case of the comparatively modern buildings of Burma, this may ordinarily be confined to (1) such plain structural repairs as will ensure the stability of the building, (2) repairs to the roof with a view to prevent the percolation of rain water, (3) earth oiling of the woodwork, when necessary to prevent the ravages of white ants, and (4) such simple protective measures as are necessary to preserve the glass incrustate work or other ornaments.

On the other hand, no pains or expense should be spared in the preservation of any woodwork belonging to the mediæval or earlier ages, as specimens of this class of work are exceedingly

4

rare and valuable, and one and all of them, whether they be complete structures like the temples of the Chamba valley, or doors, pillars and the like, built into some brick edifice, ought to be highly prized and scrupulously cared for. The treatment of such woodwork, if it is to be successful, may be a difficult and technical matter, and the assistance of the archæological officer should be sought before it is touched, particularly if it is intended to dismantle any part of it for deposit in a museum.

*Completion of work.*—Immediately after the completion of repairs to any monument, the building and its surroundings should be cleaned and tidied up. No mortar wheels, mortar heaps, brickbats or the like should be left behind.

\* \* \* \* \*

\* Our primary object is to preserve all that we can of ancient memorials and not to renovate and embellish them. The restoration of missing members is necessary in some cases for the sake of structural stability; and in some cases it is desirable for the reason that their absence seriously detracts from the beauty or symmetry of the building. But when such restorations are undertaken, they should be of the simplest and plainest kind, the mouldings or other designs being merely "blocked out" and no attempt being made to reproduce the finer details of the original work which cannot now be copied with success.

\* \* \* \* \*

A roof should not be repaired with concrete covered with white plaster which stands out in violent contrast to the grey and weather-worn walls. The new concrete or plaster should be toned down to match the colour of the masonry.

Care must, however, be taken to avoid giving too uniform a colour to the whole of the roof. This is not likely to happen, if different parts of it are repaired at different times; but, if the whole roof has to be renovated together, the Engineer in charge of the works should himself see to the mixing of the ingredients and vary their quantities a little so as to catch the different tones of the masonry below.

(b) Similarly, if it is found absolutely necessary to cement up any of the open cracks or joints in the body of a building, the cement used should invariably be treated in the same way, but I may note that the pointing of joints such as has been done all over some temples ought to be strictly forbidden. Open joints, if protected against the rain by the overhanging eaves, will do no harm, provided that jungle plants are not allowed to take root in them; and if it is really necessary to stop them, the cement should be "tucked" back about ½" or more from the surface, so as to be quite inconspicuous. It is peculiarly disfiguring to an old building, in which mortar was not originally used, to point up its joints and carelessly smear the mortar or cement over the adjoining surface.

(c) If new stone work has to be introduced for structural purposes, it should be neatly and accurately dressed. If a new stone has to replace one which was decorated with carvings, it should be merely "blocked out" so as to show the main lines or mouldings of the original, without any attempt being made to recarve the details.

(d) When the new stone work is in position its exposed surfaces should be stained to the colour of the old work adjoining with a stain made from the bean known as *semicarpus anacardium*, which is procurable in the bazaar under the name of *bhilawa* (the marking nut from which dhobies get black dic for marking linen). In order to make the stain, take 3 ozs. of the beans, put them in a mortar and pound them well. Then put in quart bottle and fill up with petrol and let the beans soak for a few days, after which the liquid can be strained off and is ready for use.

\* \* \* \* \*

The use of paraffin has been found successful on Cleopatra's needle, which is presumed to be a block of granite, and it has also been found useful as a preservative for stone fronts of buildings which are generally built either of that material or of freestone. If paraffin was found suitable on those, in the polluted atmosphere of cities in America or Europe, it should be equally effective on such stone buildings or monoliths in India, and in the crude form in which it is used for such purposes it is comparatively cheap.

\* \* \* \* \*

*A stone preserver.*—The stone preserving compound of Professor R. M. Caffall is paraffin with creosote dissolved in turpentine, and is designed primarily to protect against atmospheric action, while the paraffin prevents organic growth. This is the material with which was checked the decay of the pink granite Egyptian obelisk that was set up in New York in 1881. On its new site the obelisk began to weather rapidly and in 1885, when the protective coating was applied, 780 pounds of loose chips were removed. The heating of the surface necessary in applying the mixture—the melting point of which is 140° F.—did not have the injurious effect feared. The heat caused the substance to be absorbed to the depth of half an inch, and 67½ pounds were applied to the 200 square yards of shaft and plinth. In the 25 years since then the stone has shown no decay.

<hr>

\* Extract from the conservation notes of Mr. J. H. Marshall, Director-General of Archæology.

# APPENDIX C.

*Forms for Draft Agreements under Section 5 of Act VII of 1904.*

## I

*(For cases in which the trustee undertake to execute at their cost all ordinary repairs to the monument.)*

THIS AGREEMENT executed on the             day of        1910 between
                  , trustee of                      of             village,
             taluk,             district, hereinafter called the " trustee " which expression where
the context admits shall be deemed to include the survivor of him or other the trustee for the
time being of the said                         and his successors in office of the one part
and the Right Honourable the Secretary of State for India in Council hereinafter called the
Secretary of State which expression where the context admits shall be deemed to include his
successors in office for the time being of the other part Whereas under section 3 of the Ancient
Monuments Preservation Act (Act VII of 1904) the                        specifically
described in the schedule annexed hereto and hereinafter referred to as the " protected
monument " heretofore in the possession and management of the trustee abovenamed on behalf
of the                          has been declared by the Government of Madras to be a
protected monument under the said Act and whereas with a view to preserve the protected
monument in its present condition, the Collector of             with the previous sanction of the
Madras Government conveyed in G.O., No.         , Public, dated               , proposed to the
said trustee that he should enter into an agreement with the said Secretary of State for India
in Council for the preservation of the protected monument and the said trustee has accepted the
proposal and whereas the terms of the said agreement so proposed and accepted are embodied
in these presents and whereas those presents by G.O., No.       , dated            , have been
approved by the Government of Madras Now these presents witness that it is hereby mutually
agreed by the trustee and the said Secretary of State as follows :—

1. The trustee shall maintain the said protected monument in proper condition and repair
and agree to abide by and carry out the orders of the Madras Government and the Collector of
          for the time being as to the manner in which the same is to be preserved and as to the
repairs and all other measures that may be deemed necessary from time to time for that
purpose.

2. The trustee shall have the             under his control and make necessary arrangements
for watching the same. The trustee shall not either himself or through others destroy, remove,
alter or deface the protected monument and in particular in addition and without prejudice to
the foregoing conditions the trustee shall not construct or allow or give permission to others to
construct huts or other buildings on the site in front of or near or walls or other partitions in or
near the protected monument.

3. The trustee and his successors in office shall not allow the protected monument to be
used by any person for residential purposes.

4. The trustee shall allow all facilities for access to the protected monument to the officers
and servants of the Archæological department and also such facilities for access to the protected
monument to other officers of Government and to the public or any portion thereof at such times
and in such manner as the Collector of         for the time being may in writing require.

5. The trustee shall not sell or allow to be sold the site of the protected monument and
land to a distance of 100 feet on four sides of it.

6. The Secretary of State shall pay all expenses which may be incurred in connection with
the preservation and repair of the protected monument at the request of or under the orders of
the Collector of          for the time being or the Government of Madras But ordinary
repairs to the            periodical or otherwise shall be done at the expense of the trustee, after
approval by the Collector.

7. Subject in all respects to the foregoing conditions the trustee may with the approval of
the Collector conduct in the             such religious ceremonies as will not involve the
exclusion of persons not belonging to the Hindu community.

28

In witness whereof the said                                                     and
the Collector of            on behalf of the Secretary of State for India in Council have hereunto
set their respective hands and seals the day and year first above written.

*The schedule above referred to.*

| Name of the district, talak and village. | Description, wet or dry, with survey or palmah number. | Name of the owner. | Boundaries. | | | | Extent. |
|---|---|---|---|---|---|---|---|
| | | | North. | East. | South. | West. | |
| 1 | 2 | 3 | 4 | 5 | 6 | 7 | 8 |
| | | | | | | | |

(G.O., No. 757, Public, dated 30th August 1910.)

## II

*(For cases in which the repairs are executed at the expense of Government.)*

AGREEMENT made the            day of                    19  , between
the trustees for the time being of the                        village in the
taluk of the                district, hereinafter referred to as " the
trustees " which expression where the context admits shall be deemed to include the survivor
of them or other the trustees or trustee for the time being of the said            there and
his assigns of the one part and the RIGHT HONOURABLE THE SECRETARY OF STATE FOR INDIA
IN COUNCIL, hereinafter referred to as " the said Secretary of State " which expression where
the context admits shall be deemed to include his successors in office for the time being of the
other part.  WHEREAS under section 3 of the Ancient Monuments Preservation Act, 1904 (Act
VII of 1904), the            , specifically described in the schedule annexed hereto and hereinafter referred to as " the Protected Monument " has been declared by the Government of
Madras to be a protected monument under the said Act, AND WHEREAS with a view to preserve
the protected monument in its present condition the Collector of            with the
previous sanction of the Madras Government conveyed in G.O., No.            , dated            ,
proposed to the trustees that they should enter into an agreement with the said Secretary of
State for the preservation of the protected monument and the said trustees have accepted the
proposal.  AND WHEREAS the terms of the said agreement so proposed and accepted are embodied
in these presents.

AND WHEREAS these presents by G.O., No.            , dated            , have been
approved by the Government of Madras.  Now THESE PRESENTS WITNESS that it is hereby
mutually agreed by the trustees and the said Secretary of State as follows :—

(1) That the said Secretary of State shall have the right to maintain the protected
monument in proper condition and repair and to take any measures necessary for that purpose.

(2) That the protected monument shall be under the immediate control of the trustees.

(3) (a) That the trustees shall not either themselves or through their agents or lessees or
tenants destroy, remove, alter or deface the protected monument or any part thereof.

(b) And in particular, in addition and without prejudice to the foregoing conditions
that the trustees shall not without the previous consent in writing of the Collector of the district
construct or give permission to construct huts or other buildings on the site within the walls of
the protected monument, and shall not without such consent cultivate the said site or any part
thereof.

(4) That the trustees shall render such facilities to the public or any portion of the public
to have access to the protected monument and at such times and in such manner as the Collector
of            for the time being shall appoint.

(5) That the trustees shall render all facilities of access to the protected monument to the
Archæological Department and such other persons deputed by the Collector of            .
for the time being to inspect or maintain the protected monument.

(6) That the said Secretary of State shall pay all expenses which may be incurred in
connection with the preservation and repair of the protected monument.

(7) That in respect of the whole or any part of such expenses the said Secretary of State shall have a charge on the protected monument and on the sale-proceeds thereof in case of its sale to be realized only when the trustees effect a sale.

(8) That before offering the protected monument for sale either by public auction or private treaty, the trustees shall give to the Government of Madras six months' previous notice in writing of their intention to do so.

(9) That the said Secretary of State shall have the right to purchase the protected monument or such part of it as the said Secretary of State shall deem fit at its market value.

IN WITNESS WHEREOF the said

and the Collector of

on behalf of the Secretary of State for India in Council have hereunto set their respective hands.

*The Schedule above referred to.*

| Name of the district, taluk and village. | Description, wet or dry, with survey or paimash number. | Name of the owner. | Boundaries. | | | | Extent. |
|---|---|---|---|---|---|---|---|
| | | | North. | East. | South. | West. | |
| 1 | 2 | 3 | 4 | 5 | 6 | 7 | 8 |
| | | | | | | | |

(G.O., No. 53, Public, dated 13th January 1910.)

# APPENDIX D.

## Extracts from Government Orders.

### I

Proposals of Collectors with regard to the conservation of archæological works, should, on consultation with the Executive Engineer of the division, be made to the Superintending Engineers on or before the 1st October of each year. The Superintending Engineers should then forward a complete list to the Superintendent, Archæological Department, on or before the 1st November. If any of the officers fail to submit their estimates within the prescribed date, the Superintendent, Archæological Department, will, if necessary, bring the omission to the notice of Government. He will also furnish to Government a consolidated Conservation Budget for the whole Presidency on the 1st December. (G.Os., Nos. 347, Public, dated 12th April 1902, and 119, Public, dated 7th February 1907.)

*Submission of estimates for the repair of ancient monuments selected for conservation.*

### II

Collectors should use their influence with the managers and trustees of temples to prevent the destruction of valuable inscriptions. They should inform their Tahsildars that they will be held very strictly responsible if the contemplated destruction of any inscription is not, at once, reported to the Collector, who must see that the inscription is not interfered with at least till it has been copied. Temples of great antiquity and the details of its architecture are of value for the history of Indian Art. The inscriptions carved on stones are of great historical importance. A new temple can be built without destroying the old one, of which the trustees have good reason to be proud. (G.O., No. 1291, Public, dated 16th December 1902.)

*Reports by district officers as to the contemplated demolition or repair of ancient monuments.*

### III

The attention of all Superintending Engineers and Executive Engineers are drawn prominently to the orders laid down in Public Works Department Code, volume I, paragraphs 300, 301 and 897, and they should take every opportunity of performing their duty in respect to the preservation of monuments of archæological interest. (G.O., No. 1650 W., dated 9th June 1903.)

*Care and upkeep of ancient monuments. Duties of Public Works Department Officers.*

## Extract from the Public Works Department Code, 1907.

300. It is the duty of an Executive Engineer to suggest public improvements, and to prepare detailed designs for them, as far as he may be able to do so without permitting any interference with the prosecution of those designs or works specially ordered by superior departmental authority. In provinces where there is no Archæological Officer, he is also required to report on, and suggest measures for, the protection of any public monument or building of architectural or historical interest, which appears likely to fall into decay, and he will be responsible for any neglect or destruction which he has failed to report—see also paragraph 897.

301. The term " public monument or building of architectural or historical interest " above is intended to include all works of this class whether public or private property. In the latter case it will be for the Local Government to decide whether the Government shall take any further steps than those of endeavouring to influence the owners.

897. All buildings and monuments of historical or architectural interest should be carefully attended to, and where no Archæological Officer exists it will be the duty of Executive and Superintending Engineers to keep Government fully informed as to their condition and to prepare estimates for repairs. In provinces where an Archæological Superintendent of Surveys exists it will be the duty of the latter —

(1) To advise on the proposals for conservation or restoration works submitted by the officers of the Public Works Department, and to recommend the order of precedence, in which these as well as any works suggested by themselves should be undertaken.

(2) To submit proposals for the conservation or repair of ancient buildings of interest requiring preservation which have come to their own notice during their tours. This work should be carried out *pari passu* with the preparation of the list of remains referred to in Government of India, Home Department Circular No. 12–28, dated 21th August 1891, where these have not yet been completed and should not await their final completion.

(3) To pass plans and estimates for all works of conservation and repair whether suggested by himself or by the Public Works Department. It will not be the duty of the Archæological Officer to criticise rates, but to approve and advise on the character of the works to be carried out.

(4) To assist in the supervision of the works of conservation while they are in progress. The degree of assistance required must depend upon the nature and importance of the work. It will be the duty of the Archæological Officer to assist the Engineer with his advice and to bring to the notice of the proper authority any alterations or repairs, which, in his opinion, are likely to affect the architectural interest of the building—*see* also paragraphs 300 and 301.

## IV

The duties of the Provincial Archæological Officers are—

Duties of Archæological Officers.

(1) To advise on the proposals for conservation or restoration works submitted by the officers of the Public Works Department, and to recommend the order of precedence, in which these as well as any works suggested by themselves should be undertaken.

(2) To submit proposals for the conservation or repair of ancient buildings of interest requiring preservation which have come to their own notice during their tours. This work should be carried out *pari passu* with the preparation of the list of remains referred to in the Government of India Circular No. 12–28, dated 24th August 1891, where these have not yet been completed and should not await their final completion.

(3) To pass plans and estimates for all works of conservation and repair whether suggested by himself or by the Public Works Department. It will not be the duty of the Archæological Officer to criticise rates, but to approve and advise on the character of the works to be carried out.

(4) To assist in the supervision of the works of conservation while they are in progress. The degree of assistance required must depend upon the nature and importance of the work. It will be the duty of the Archæological Officer to assist the Engineer with his advice and to bring to the notice of the proper authority any alterations or repairs, which, in his opinion, are likely to affect the architectural or historical interest of the building.

The manner and extent to which these duties are carried out by Archæological Officers should be clearly stated in the first section of their annual progress reports. It should be understood that, in prescribing them, the Government of India do not intend to relieve Public Works officers of the responsibility which also rests upon them. It is impossible for an Archæological Surveyor to make regular or systematic inspections of all the monuments in the large areas under his charge, and this duty will rest as heretofore primarily with the Public Works Department, who should endeavour to arrange for a systematic annual, or even more frequent, inspection to be made by Executive Engineers of the monuments in their circles. But notice of any measures which may be suggested by officers of the Public Works Department for the protection or conservation of any monument should invariably be communicated to the Provincial Archæological Officer before they are carried out, in order that he may have an opportunity of expressing his opinion as to their suitability. Similarly no repairs or removal of ancient buildings or remains should be undertaken by District or Municipal authorities without previous report to the Provincial Archæological Officer, who should also be kept informed of any intended demolition or defacement of ancient buildings, inscriptions, or other antiquities in private possession which may come to their knowledge. (Resolution of the Government of India, Department of Revenue and Agriculture, Archæology and Epigraphy, dated 7th July 1903, No. 26–28—2 printed in G.O., No. 745, Public, dated 21st August 1903.)

## V

Periodical inspection of ancient monuments by officers of the Public Works Department.

All ancient monuments selected for conservation should be inspected annually by officers of the Public Works Department. No repairs or removals of ancient buildings or remains should be undertaken without previous reference to the Superintendent, Archæological Department. All Collectors should see that the Superintendent, Archæological Department, is kept informed of any intended demolition or defacement of ancient buildings, inscriptions or other antiquities in private possession which may come to their knowledge and that no excavation of ancient sites or mounds are permitted until the consent of Government has been obtained thereto. (G.O., No. 745, Public, dated 21st August 1903.)

5-A

## 32

## VI

**Proposals for the repair at public expense of ancient monuments likely to be resumed for worship.** Whenever proposals are submitted to Government for the restoration or repair at the public expense of an ancient building, which is likely to be claimed after restoration for the resumption in it of worship, the officer making the proposals should suggest for the consideration of Government, conditions suitable to the local circumstances to be attached to the restoration of the building. Such conditions should provide either for its permanent reservation as an historical or architectural monument or if it is proposed to permit the resumption of worship in it for its preservation from ruin through neglect, for its being kept not less open than before for public inspection and for it resumption by Government should it relapse into a state of disrepair and disfigurement, or should other conditions not be fulfilled. (G.O., No. 790, Public, dated 4th September 1903.)

## VII

**Reports on the condition of ancient monuments by Superintending Engineers.** Under existing orders Superintending Engineers submit to the Chief Engineer, Public Works Department, on or before the 15th April in each year, reports on the condition of ancient monuments in their circles, but these reports, in many cases, do not include all the selected monuments in each circle, but merely mention such of them as are considered to need repair, blank reports being frequently submitted. The reports are forwarded, through the Public Works and Public departments, to the Superintendent, Archæological Survey.

2. In future the reports should contain a list of all the selected monuments in each circle arranged according to the numbers in the standard list and should be in the same form as the standard list. The last three columns of the report should show the date on which each monument was inspected, the designation of the officer by whom it was inspected, its condition, any measures of conservation carried out during the year and any further measures which are considered necessary. The reports should reach the Superintendent, Archæological Survey, sufficiently early in the year to admit of the information being embodied in his annual report which is due with the Government on the 15th of June. It is unnecessary that they should be transmitted to the Superintendent through two departments of the Government, and they will therefore be forwarded by Superintending Engineers direct to the Superintendent, Archæological Survey, so as to reach the latter officer on or before the 15th of April each year. (G.O., No 1158, Public, dated the 23rd December 1903.)

## VIII

### DEMOLITION OF ANCIENT MONUMENTS IN THE CUSTODY OF PRIVATE INDIVIDUALS.

#### 1.—*Memorandum by A. REA, Esq., F.S.A. (SCOT.), M.R.A.S., Superintendent, Archæological Survey.*

1. Much can be done by the influence of local officials, in the way of preventing destruction or demolition to ancient monuments of archæological interest in the possession of private individuals. In the case of local influence failing to do so, all that can be done is the copying of the inscriptions and the photographing of the building.

In this connection I would reiterate what I have expressed as my views in such matters, in my letter to Government No. 577, dated 10th September 1903. The destruction by Nattukottai Chetties of the temple therein mentioned is no doubt done through pious though mistaken motives, and with the intention of erecting on its site a new building,—perhaps considered more suitable—in its stead, as has been done by others at Jambukesvaram and many other places. It might be pointed out, however, that in all ages in India, kings and other benefactors have made grants and additions to temples and built others, but I do not know that it was ever considered necessary to first destroy existing shrines. Such work has hitherto been confined to the followers of opposing sects or other religions. Thus many of what are now the largest South Indian temples were originally only small shrines of perhaps Chola date. External additions of courts, gopurams, etc., successively made by the kings of Vijayanagar and the Madura Nayaks, left them what they now are. The Nattukottai Chetties, by following such an example, would still be able to carry out their pious wishes, without destroying the architectural works and historical records of these earlier benefactors. If the present destruction continues, it is only a question of time for the most interesting parts of the most important temples to entirely disappear, their places being taken by modern structures of no value whatever. If, instead of demolishing buildings which are already in a more or less perfect state of preservation, and then rebuilding them anew, they devoted themselves to the repair of sacred shrines actually needing it, nothing could be urged against such good work.

Railway Engineers and contractors might also be included, for in the course of opening new lines, some pre-historic or other sites might be destroyed without any notice being given to the authorities; and when these officers do come across such sites, it is desirable that they at once bring it to the notice of the Government.

Such a procedure will obviate all wanton destruction which might now be carried on, without the knowledge of the Archæological department.

Instances of such demolition or destruction which are brought to the notice of the Archæological department, at present, are very few; and it is generally a matter of chance when such are heard of.

*11.—Extract from letter No. 522, dated 29th October 1903, from M.R.Ry. V. VENKAYYA Avargal, M.A., Officiating Government Epigraphist, to the Chief Secretary to Government.*

    •    •    •    •    •

4. When reliable information about repairs to an ancient building has been obtained, the subsequent procedure is not very complicated. The Collector concerned will send for the trustee and persuade him not to pull down existing shrines which do not require any repairs but to erect, if necessary, new ones which would be more meritorious. If the trustee is not willing to listen to any such advices, the matter may be dropped and an attempt made to save all the inscribed stones and those containing sculptures worthy of preservation. So far as experience goes, not much use is made of old stones in rebuilding temples. Perhaps they are utilised in laying the foundations of new walls. Consequently all traces of them are lost. No hardship will be caused to temple trustees, who spend several lakhs of rupees in rebuilding a temple, if they are prevented absolutely from making any use of old stones which bear writing. Thus, it cannot be very difficult to secure the inscribed stones of a shrine or wall that has been pulled down. The best course to be adopted after securing the stones is to number them and set them up in the temple itself or in some other convenient and safe locality. This the trustees generally promise to do, but experience has proved that their numbering is very defective and that the stones are never set up in any order. It is, therefore, necessary that this should be done at the expense of Government and under the joint supervision of the Archæological and Public Works departments. Any funds which the Government can allot for conservation of ancient monuments cannot, in my opinion, be better spent than in setting up in some order the inscribed stones of a temple that has been pulled down. If inscribed stones are allowed to be used in building new shrines, special care must be taken that clauses 8, 10, 12 and 13 of the memorandum are strictly enforced.

5. The repair or rebuilding of a big temple generally takes several years, and I would suggest, as an additional precaution, that Archæological officers should visit such temples as frequently as possible—say not less than twice a year. This is necessary to prevent disappearance of stones possessing any antiquarian interest. When ancient shrines are being pulled down, inscriptions which had been built in or otherwise inaccessible may be easily copied. Inscribed stones utilised in previous restorations may also turn up. These may be secured without any trouble, if an Archæological Officer is present on the spot.

6. A perfectly barbarous practice, in which the Nattukottai Chetties indulge while repairing temples, requires also to be put down. When they do not pull down a building, they chisel away any writing that may be found on its walls in order to make them white and smooth. They have done this in Tiruvannâmalai and Tiruvennanallûr and thus wantonly destroyed a large number of valuable inscriptions. They proposed to do the same with the inscriptions on the walls of the central shrine in the temple at Kâlahasti. I tried my best to dissuade them by saying that inscriptions recorded acts of charity in the past and it would be a sin to destroy them. But I am not sure if they will leave these inscriptions untouched. It ought in the first instance to be the interest of the trustees to prevent this fresh vandalic idea of the Nattukottai Chetties. Clause 13 of the memorandum is intended to check this practice. Mainly to secure this end and generally to restrain the vandalic propensities of temple trustees and Nattukottai Chetties, they must be required to enter into a written agreement with the Collector that they will strictly observe the clauses of the memorandum which apply to them. The agreement will, in most cases, not have to be enforced at all, because the periodical visits of Archæological officers, . . . . and the moral effect of the written agreement will be quite enough for all practical purposes to effectively keep down any tendency to break the clauses of the memorandum.

7. I take advantage of this opportunity to bring to the notice of Government an objectionable practice of temple trustees. Every year the walls of temples are whitewashed at considerable expense during festivals. In many ancient shrines I have found the walls covered with a thick layer of chunam which damages them and eventually destroys the inscriptions engraved on them. District officers may also be requested to use their influence in putting a stop to this practice which benefits nobody.

### III.—Memorandum by M.R.Ry. V. VENKAYYA Avargal, M.A.

    •       •       •       •

On receiving a report of any intended repairs to a temple, the Collector will communicate with the nearest Public Works department officer who should be asked to inspect the temple or other building which is proposed to be repaired and to state if any repairs are actually required or not. In the former case, the Public Works department officer will also suggest how the alterations may be executed without seriously interfering with the existing buildings or without impairing their antiquarian value.

The Collector will then send for the trustee, who may be informed of the contents of the circular issued by the Royal Asiatic Society. The trustee should be told that inscriptions record endowments to temples and pious individuals and that it is meritorious to preserve such records. He should be exhorted not to interfere with the existing buildings in case they do not require any repairs, but to build fresh shrines in the same temple, if necessary. In case repairs are required, the suggestions of the Public Works department officer, who inspected the temple, may be placed before the trustee for acceptance.

If the trustee insists in pulling down the existing buildings he may be asked to wait until the Archæological officers are communicated with.

Before beginning to pull down existing buildings, the trustee should be required to enter into an agreement (perhaps with the Collector of the district) that he will abide by clauses 8, 12 and 13 of this memorandum and that, in default thereof, he will render himself liable to prosecution for mischief under sections 425 and 426 of the Indian Penal Code.

As soon as possible after receiving intimation of the intended demolition of a temple, the Government Epigraphist will copy all the inscriptions found on its walls and the Superintendent, Archæological Survey, will take photographs and plaster casts wherever necessary.

While repairs are going on, Archæological officers will visit the temple as often as possible to see that nothing of antiquarian interest disappears.

Stones of any antiquarian value should not be used in erecting fresh shrines—particularly in laying foundations of new walls. This restriction is also applicable to old stones discovered or unearthed in the course of repairs.

Any of these stones which may be particularly valuable from an archæological point of view must be acquired for the Government Central Museum, Madras.

The rest must be arranged in some order in the temple itself or in some other place where they would not suffer damage in any way.

Stones disposed of under clause (10) should be treated in the same way as temple or other building selected for conservation.

If inscribed stones are to be used at all in the new buildings, they must be set up in the same order in which they originally stood. To ensure this the person in charge of the repairs may be directed to regulate his operations in such a way that the setting up of inscribed stones is taken up on a definite date, of which the Government Epigraphist must have previous notice, and finished within a reasonable time. As masons generally insert stones according to their own convenience, they must not be allowed to handle inscribed stones except in the presence of experts. They must be prohibited particularly from chopping off inscribed stones as they like.

Neither the trustee, nor any person acting under his orders shall interfere in any way with the inscribed stones belonging to those portions of a temple which are not intended to be repaired.

    •       •       •       •

ORDER—No. 43, Public, dated 16th January 1904.

The memoranda above read will be communicated to all Collectors who will be requested to act upon the suggestions contained therein so far as may be practicable.

    •       •       •       •

As already directed in G.O., No. 1291, Public, dated the 16th December 1902, Collectors should use their personal influence to prevent the destruction of valuable inscriptions, and should communicate to the owners or trustees of temples which are about to be reconstructed the letter of the Royal Asiatic Society on the subject; and Tahsildars should bring promptly to the notice of the Collector any contemplated destruction of an ancient building containing inscriptions.

### IX

Government will be prepared to consider any proposals which are submitted through the Superintendent, Archæological Department, for the conservation of ancient monuments not included in the selected list. All Collectors should use their influence when the reconstruction of an ancient temple cannot be prevented, to persuade the trustees or owners to have the work carried out under the skilled advice of the Superintendent, Archæological Department, and the Government Epigraphist. (G.O., No. 290, Public, dated 29th March 1904.)

*Conservation of monuments not included in the selected list.*

## 35

## X

When temples are possessed of large revenues, then it is obvious no grant is necessary from
*Inspection or repair of ancient buildings which are either private property or in use for worship.*
Government and only advice is needed to be given to them if they wish it. When their funds are insufficient a proportional grant can be made by Government or the whole expenditure may be so paid.

When any building the inspection of which has been suggested by the Superintendent of the Archæological Department, is private property or in use for worship, it will be sufficient if, in the first instance, the Superintendent is furnished by the officer of the Public Works Department concerned with a report on its general state of repair. It will then rest with the Superintendent, Archæological Department, to decide after enquiry whether advice should be given to the owner, or custodian of the building, or action should be taken under Act 7 of 1904, or proposal should be made to the Government for a proportionate grant-in-aid of the repairs which may be considered necessary. (G.O., No. 754, Public, dated 2nd September 1904.)

## XI

Whenever it is considered necessary by any officer of Government to remove any struc-
*Removal of structures of archæological interest.*
tures which appear to be old and may be of archæological interest, the Superintendent, Archæological Department, should invariably be consulted before any steps are taken for their removal. (G.O., No. 211, Public, dated 19th March 1906).

## XII

As a general rule the Government do not consider it necessary that ancient monuments
*Application of Act VII of 1904.*
which are the property of Government should be declared to be " protected monuments " under section 3 (1) of the Ancient Monuments Preservation Act, 1904 (VII of 1904). (G.O., No. 438, Public, dated 10th June 1906).

All ancient monuments which are the property of Government and included in the list of monuments selected for conservation are in the charge of the Public Works Department. Every such monument must be inspected at least once a year by an officer of the Public Works Department and its condition reported The duties of officers of the Public Works Department in respect to buildings of historical or architectural interest are further defined in paragraphs 300, 301 and 897 of the Public Works Code quoted at page 30.

The Ancient Monuments Preservation Act VII of 1904, was designed chiefly to protect from damage or destruction of ancient monuments which are private property. Government Order No. 438, Public, dated the 10th June 1906, enumerates a general principle with regard to monuments which are Government property. In the case of such monuments the Superintendent of Archæological Department, wherever he deems it proper to do so, should have a board put up warning the people that the monument is Government property and that no sculpture, carving, or any stone, shall be removed from the site. In special cases, a notification will be issued by Government under section 18 of the Act, but ordinarily a simple intimation of the former description will probably suffice. (G.O., No. 516, Public, dated 12th July 1906.)

## XIII

The Officers of the Revenue and Public Works Departments should see that the injunc-
*Vegetation on ancient monuments.*
tions contained in the following memorandum are brought to the notice of the custodians of ancient monuments :—

### *Prevention of Growth of Vegetation on Ancient Monuments.*

That vegetation plays an active part in the destruction of temples and other ancient monuments is a fact very well known. It is one of the chief destructive influences in a tropical climate. But the custodians of ancient monuments do not, as a rule, seem to take any notice of these growths on the walls, either when they are but small plants, or even after they are deeply rooted, and consequently buildings are damaged to such an extent that heavy sums have to be sent in their restoration, though no renovation can restore the original beauty of the structure.

Some custodians do make a show of removing the leaves and stems leaving the root to again produce a new and probably more luxuriant growth than before, and as the roots expand with the growth of the plants, the masonry, however heavy and solid it may be, is invariably forced out of position, and, if not checked in time, will ultimately fall into ruin. All this could be avoided at little or no expense by the removal of young plants whenever they appear in any joints of the masonry.

The attention of the custodians of ancient monuments should be drawn to the fact, that the first and foremost duty to be done in preserving such buildings is the constant removal of such growths to the very end of the root, and the application immediately thereafter of *scrub eradicator.* *

That the ancient Hindus were not unaware of the evil effects of vegetation is evident from the fact that, in many important temples, due provision has been made in the accounts for the annual clearance of vegetation, though, in practice, it is not now done in the manner in which it should and ought to be done, and is in most cases neglected.

Touring officers of the Revenue and Public Works departments should make it a point to bring these to the notice of the custodians of all ancient monuments, and also note the action taken in this connection in their diaries to their superiors. In the worst cases, where there is any probability of any part of a building collapsing from this cause, a special report may be made to the Collector of the district, who would do well to bring it to the notice of the Archæological Department. (G.O., No. 802, Public, dated 3rd September 1910.)